Paying Off Your Mortgage with Rental Income and House Hacking

How to Use Real Estate Cash Flow to Cover and Eliminate Your Mortgage

By Joseph G. Correa

Copyright & Legal Notice

Published by Live Stronger Faster

First Edition, 2026

Table of Contents

Introduction

For many homeowners, the mortgage is the single largest financial obligation they will ever carry. It often represents decades of payments, thousands of dollars in interest, and a long-term commitment that can feel both necessary and overwhelming. While owning a home can create stability, pride, and long-term wealth, the mortgage attached to that home can also become one of the biggest obstacles standing between a family and true financial freedom. Month after month, year after year, many people wake up knowing a large portion of their income is already spoken for before they even begin paying for groceries, transportation, healthcare, travel, education, or investments. The mortgage becomes a permanent fixture in life, and many people assume this is simply how life must be. Yet there is another path available—one that allows homeowners to use real estate itself as the solution to eliminating the mortgage faster than they ever thought possible.

This book is about that path. It is about using rental income and house hacking strategies to transform your property from a monthly expense into a financial asset that actively works to eliminate debt, accelerate equity growth, and create long-term financial flexibility. Rather than relying only on salary increases, bonuses, or strict budgeting to pay off a mortgage, this strategy uses cash flow generated from real estate to attack the mortgage balance while simultaneously creating opportunities for wealth expansion. It allows homeowners to rethink the role of their home entirely. Instead of seeing the property as something that drains money every month, they begin to see it as an income-producing machine capable of generating freedom, security, and opportunity.

Many people mistakenly believe that real estate investing requires large amounts of money, dozens of properties, or years of experience. In reality, some of the most powerful wealth-building strategies begin with a single property and a willingness to think differently about how that property can be used. House hacking has become one of the most effective modern strategies for homeowners who want to reduce or eliminate their housing costs while accelerating financial growth. The concept is simple yet incredibly powerful. By renting out portions of a property—whether that means individual rooms, a basement, an accessory dwelling unit, a duplex, or even a vacation rental space—a homeowner can generate income that offsets or completely covers the monthly mortgage payment. In some cases, homeowners are able to live nearly payment-free while building equity and watching tenants gradually help pay off the loan balance. The beauty of this strategy is that it works for people across many different income levels and lifestyles. A young professional purchasing a duplex may live in one unit while renting the other. A family may convert part of their home into a separate rental suite. Someone living near a university may rent rooms to students. A homeowner in a tourist-heavy area may use short-term rental platforms to create additional cash flow. Others may buy small multifamily properties with owner-occupied financing and dramatically reduce their living expenses while gaining experience as real estate investors. The possibilities are enormous because the strategy is flexible, scalable, and adaptable to changing financial goals.

One of the greatest financial advantages of house hacking and rental income strategies is leverage. Most people work only through active income, meaning they exchange time for money. Yet real estate creates the opportunity for passive or semi-passive income streams that continue generating revenue long after the initial setup is complete. When rental income is directed strategically toward the mortgage balance, the results can become life-changing. A mortgage that originally seemed impossible to pay off early may suddenly begin shrinking rapidly. Interest expenses decline. Equity builds faster. Cash flow improves. Financial stress decreases. Most importantly, the homeowner gains options and control over their future.

This book is not about unrealistic promises or overnight success. It is not about becoming a millionaire instantly or buying dozens of properties within a year. Instead, it focuses on practical, achievable strategies that ordinary people can use to reduce financial pressure and accelerate long-term wealth creation. Many homeowners already possess untapped opportunities within the property they currently own. Others may be preparing to buy their first home and want to structure the purchase intelligently from the beginning. Regardless of where you are in your financial journey, the principles in this book are designed to help you maximize the power of your property.

One reason so many people struggle financially despite having decent incomes is because their housing costs consume too much of their monthly cash flow. Mortgage payments, property taxes, insurance, maintenance, utilities, and repairs can create tremendous pressure. Even high-income earners can become trapped when too much income goes toward housing expenses instead of investments, savings, or business opportunities. Rental income changes the equation by helping offset those obligations. Instead of one income source carrying the full burden of the mortgage, multiple income streams begin supporting the property. This creates financial breathing room that can dramatically accelerate debt reduction and wealth accumulation. Throughout this book, you will discover how to identify opportunities for generating rental income even if you currently own only one property. You will learn how to evaluate different types of rental strategies, including long-term rentals, short-term rentals, room rentals, multifamily properties, and accessory dwelling units. You will understand how to analyze cash flow, estimate expenses, calculate potential returns, and determine whether a property can help accelerate mortgage payoff goals. Most importantly, you will learn how to align these strategies with your personal lifestyle and financial objectives.

Many homeowners fear becoming landlords because they imagine constant maintenance problems, difficult tenants, legal complications, or overwhelming responsibilities. While real estate certainly requires management and planning, much of the fear surrounding rental properties comes from lack of knowledge and preparation. The truth is that systems, technology, proper screening, and strong financial planning can simplify many aspects of property management. In addition, the rewards often far outweigh the challenges when properties are managed correctly. Rental income not only helps eliminate mortgage debt but can eventually create recurring monthly cash flow that supports future investments, retirement goals, travel, or financial independence.

Another major advantage of using rental income to pay off a mortgage is inflation protection. Over time, rents often rise while fixed-rate mortgage payments remain relatively stable. This means that a property purchased today may become increasingly profitable over the years as rental income grows. What may initially cover only part of the mortgage payment could eventually cover the entire payment and generate surplus cash flow beyond that. Meanwhile, the mortgage balance continues declining as tenants indirectly help pay down the debt. This creates a powerful long-term wealth-building effect that many homeowners fail to fully appreciate when they first purchase property.

House hacking also provides one of the most accessible entry points into real estate investing because it often allows buyers to use owner-occupied financing. Owner-occupied loans generally require lower down payments, offer lower interest rates, and provide more favorable qualification standards than traditional investment property loans. This means individuals can enter the world of real estate investing sooner and with less capital than they originally believed possible. Instead of waiting years to save large down payments for investment properties, many people can begin building wealth immediately by strategically purchasing a home designed to generate income from day one.

Financial freedom is not always about making more money. Often, it is about reducing financial obligations and increasing control over your monthly expenses. A homeowner whose mortgage is mostly covered by rental income experiences a completely different level of financial flexibility compared to someone fully dependent on a paycheck to cover housing costs. Job loss becomes less catastrophic. Career changes become easier. Entrepreneurship becomes more realistic. Travel becomes more possible. Retirement planning improves dramatically. The emotional and psychological benefits of reducing mortgage pressure are just as important as the mathematical benefits.

One of the most important lessons you will learn in this book is that your home can become a financial partner instead of merely a liability. Many people buy homes based entirely on emotion without considering how the property could support their long-term financial future. They purchase homes that maximize expenses rather than opportunities. By contrast, financially intelligent homeowners evaluate how a property can generate income, reduce costs, and create future flexibility. This shift in mindset alone can transform the trajectory of a family's finances over the next several decades.

As you progress through this book, you will also learn about balancing mortgage payoff with wealth creation. In some cases, aggressively paying off a mortgage as fast as possible may not always produce the best overall financial outcome. Strategic investors understand that cash flow, leverage, appreciation, and tax advantages can work together to create larger long-term gains. The goal is not simply eliminating debt blindly. The goal is maximizing financial strength, flexibility, and long-term security while minimizing unnecessary risk.

You will also discover how different markets, property types, financing structures, and economic conditions affect rental strategies and mortgage acceleration. Real estate is not one-size-fits-all. A successful strategy for one homeowner may look completely different for another. Someone living in a high-tourism market may benefit from short-term rentals, while another homeowner may achieve stronger stability through long-term tenants or room rentals. Understanding how to adapt these strategies intelligently is critical to long-term success.

This book was created to provide practical guidance, strategic insight, and financial inspiration for homeowners who want more from their property than simple ownership alone. Whether your goal is eliminating your mortgage in ten years instead of thirty, reducing financial stress, building investment capital, creating passive income, or achieving complete financial independence, rental income and house hacking can become powerful tools to help you reach those objectives faster.

The journey toward mortgage freedom often begins with a simple realization: your property has the potential to generate income, not just consume it. Once you understand how to unlock that potential, everything changes. The mortgage no longer feels like a lifelong burden. Instead, it becomes a challenge that can be systematically reduced using strategy, discipline, creativity, and intelligent real estate planning.

By the end of this book, you will see your home differently. You will understand how ordinary properties can create extraordinary financial leverage when approached strategically. You will gain insight into how countless homeowners have used rental income and house hacking to accelerate mortgage payoff timelines, build equity rapidly, and create lasting wealth. Most importantly, you will realize that financial freedom is often much closer than most people imagine when they learn how to make real estate work for them instead of against them.

Chapter 1

Understanding the Power of Rental Income and House Hacking

For most homeowners, the mortgage payment represents one of the largest and most stressful monthly financial obligations they will ever face. Every month, money leaves their bank account to cover principal, interest, property taxes, insurance, and maintenance costs, often leaving little room for investing, saving, or building additional streams of income. Many people accept this reality as unavoidable because they believe homeownership automatically means decades of heavy financial responsibility. However, what many homeowners fail to realize is that the same property creating financial pressure can also become the solution to reducing that pressure. A home does not need to function only as a place to live. It can also become a source of income, a wealth-building tool, and a financial accelerator capable of dramatically reducing or eliminating the mortgage much faster than originally planned.

The foundation of this strategy begins with understanding rental income and house hacking. House hacking is one of the most practical and accessible wealth-building techniques available to everyday homeowners. At its core, house hacking means using part of your property to generate income while you live in the property yourself. This can include renting out extra bedrooms, converting a basement or garage into a rental space, living in one side of a duplex while renting the other side, purchasing a triplex or fourplex with owner-occupied financing, or even renting portions of the property on short-term rental platforms. The objective is simple but powerful: use rental income to offset housing expenses and accelerate financial growth.

Many people incorrectly assume that real estate investing is only for wealthy individuals or experienced investors. In reality, house hacking allows ordinary people to begin building wealth with the property they already own or plan to purchase. A single property can become the beginning of long-term financial freedom when managed strategically. The homeowner benefits from appreciation, loan paydown, tax advantages, and rental income simultaneously. Instead of carrying the full burden of the mortgage alone, tenants help cover the debt. This changes the entire financial structure of homeownership.

One of the reasons house hacking has become increasingly popular is because housing costs continue rising across many areas of the country. Mortgage payments, insurance premiums, taxes, maintenance costs, utilities, and interest rates have placed tremendous pressure on homeowners. At the same time, wages in many industries have not increased at the same pace as living expenses. As a result, many families feel financially trapped despite owning homes. Rental income provides a practical solution by introducing additional cash flow without necessarily requiring a second full-time job. In some situations, rental income can reduce housing expenses by hundreds or even thousands of dollars per month. Over time, those savings can be redirected toward additional mortgage payments, investments, emergency savings, or retirement accounts.

The concept of using real estate to reduce financial pressure is not new. Wealthy individuals have been using income-producing properties for generations to build financial security and long-term wealth. What has changed is that modern technology, financing options, and rental platforms have made these strategies more accessible than ever before. Today, someone with a single-family home can generate income through room rentals, accessory dwelling units, or short-term rental platforms. A first-time buyer can purchase a duplex with a low down payment and allow tenants to help pay the mortgage. A family can strategically redesign unused space in their property to create additional income streams. The opportunities are far more flexible than many people realize.

One of the greatest benefits of house hacking is that it reduces the largest expense category for most households: housing. Financial freedom becomes much easier when housing costs are minimized. Imagine a homeowner with a $3,000 monthly mortgage payment who generates $2,000 per month from rental income. Instead of carrying the full payment burden personally, the homeowner now effectively pays only $1,000 out of pocket. If the homeowner applies additional savings or income toward the principal balance, the mortgage payoff timeline can accelerate dramatically. This creates a compounding effect because each extra payment reduces future interest expenses while increasing equity growth.

Equity is one of the most important concepts in real estate wealth building. Equity represents the difference between the property's value and the remaining mortgage balance. Every mortgage payment gradually increases equity as the loan balance declines. Property appreciation can also increase equity as home values rise over time. When rental income helps cover mortgage payments, equity grows faster because the homeowner can allocate more personal income toward principal reduction or other investments. Over several years, this can create a substantial increase in net worth.

Another major advantage of house hacking is the ability to enter real estate investing with owner-occupied financing.

Traditional investment properties often require larger down payments, higher interest rates, and stricter qualification standards. However, owner-occupied properties usually offer lower down payment requirements and more favorable financing terms. This means someone can purchase a duplex, triplex, or fourplex while living in one unit and renting the others. Instead of waiting years to save for investment properties, homeowners can begin building a real estate portfolio much sooner.

The psychological impact of reducing housing costs should not be underestimated. Financial stress affects relationships, mental health, career decisions, and overall quality of life. Many homeowners feel trapped because their mortgage payment consumes too much of their monthly income. House hacking can create financial breathing room that changes everything. A homeowner with reduced housing expenses may feel more comfortable starting a business, changing careers, traveling, investing, or spending more time with family. Financial flexibility often creates opportunities that would otherwise feel impossible.

One common fear people have about rental income strategies is privacy. Some homeowners hesitate because they do not want tenants living in their space. However, house hacking strategies can be customized based on comfort level and property structure. Some people rent spare bedrooms while sharing common areas. Others create fully separate living spaces with private entrances. Duplexes, garage apartments, detached guest houses, and basement suites allow homeowners to maintain greater separation while still generating income. The key is designing a setup that supports both financial goals and personal lifestyle preferences.

Another fear involves property management and dealing with tenants. While managing rental property requires responsibility, many problems can be reduced through proper tenant screening, clear lease agreements, communication, and planning. In addition, many homeowners begin with long-term tenants or carefully selected roommates before expanding into more advanced rental strategies. Experience grows over time, and systems become easier to manage. What initially feels intimidating often becomes routine after proper preparation and education.

Short-term rentals have also created new opportunities for homeowners seeking additional cash flow. Platforms like Airbnb and VRBO allow homeowners to rent rooms, guest houses, or portions of properties to travelers. In some markets, short-term rental income can significantly exceed traditional long-term rental income. However, short-term rentals also require additional management, cleaning, regulation compliance, and customer service. The decision between long-term and short-term rental strategies depends on local laws, market demand, personal availability, and financial goals.

Cash flow is the lifeblood of any successful rental strategy. Positive cash flow occurs when rental income exceeds the total property expenses, including mortgage payments, taxes, insurance, maintenance, utilities, vacancy reserves, and management costs. Even modest positive cash flow can dramatically improve financial stability over time. More importantly, excess cash flow can be redirected toward additional principal payments to accelerate mortgage payoff.

For example, imagine a homeowner with a $350,000 mortgage who receives an additional $1,500 per month from rental income. If even a portion of that income is consistently applied toward the principal balance, the homeowner may eliminate years from the mortgage term while saving tens or even hundreds of thousands of dollars in interest. The combination of rental income and accelerated principal reduction creates a powerful wealth-building engine.

One of the most overlooked aspects of house hacking is lifestyle design. Many people think financial freedom requires sacrificing enjoyment or living in extreme discomfort. In reality, house hacking often provides flexibility and opportunities that improve lifestyle quality over time. Temporary sacrifices can create long-term rewards. Someone may choose to rent rooms for several years in exchange for becoming mortgage-free much earlier in life. Another homeowner may purchase a small multifamily property, reduce living expenses dramatically, and later transition into additional investments. The short-term inconvenience can create decades of financial advantage.

Location also plays a major role in successful rental strategies. Areas near universities, hospitals, business centers, tourist destinations, beaches, or growing employment markets often provide strong rental demand. Understanding local market trends helps homeowners identify opportunities to maximize occupancy and rental income. At the same time, homeowners must carefully evaluate zoning laws, homeowner association rules, licensing requirements, insurance needs, and local regulations before implementing rental strategies.

This book will guide you through these concepts step by step. You will learn how to evaluate properties, calculate cash flow, estimate rental demand, understand financing options, manage risks, and create long-term mortgage payoff strategies using rental income. Most importantly, you will begin developing the mindset necessary to view your property not merely as a monthly expense, but as an asset capable of generating freedom and wealth.

The difference between financially stressed homeowners and financially successful homeowners often comes down to strategy. Many people buy homes emotionally without considering income potential. Others intentionally purchase or structure properties to create cash flow and financial leverage. Over time, those decisions compound dramatically. A property that generates income can become the foundation for paying off debt, investing in additional real estate, funding retirement, or creating generational wealth.

The truth is that many homeowners are far closer to financial freedom than they realize. They simply have not yet learned how to unlock the earning potential of the property they already possess. Once rental income begins reducing mortgage pressure, the homeowner gains momentum. Financial confidence increases. Equity grows faster. Opportunities expand. The mortgage balance begins shrinking more aggressively. What once felt like a lifelong burden slowly transforms into a manageable challenge with a clear path toward elimination.

House hacking is not merely about saving money. It is about transforming the financial role of your home entirely. Instead of working endlessly to support the property, the property begins supporting you. That shift changes everything. It changes how you think about debt, income, investing, risk, and long-term wealth creation. It allows homeowners to stop seeing themselves as trapped by housing expenses and start seeing themselves as strategic operators capable of building lasting financial freedom through intelligent real estate decisions.

The journey toward mortgage freedom through rental income begins with a single decision: choosing to see your home differently. Once you understand the power of leveraging real estate cash flow, you realize that the mortgage no longer needs to dominate your financial life for the next thirty years. With strategy, discipline, creativity, and consistency, your property can become one of the most powerful financial tools you will ever own.

The Duplex That Changed Everything

When Daniel purchased his first home, he believed he had finally achieved the American dream. At thirty-two years old, he had worked hard for nearly a decade to save enough money for a down payment. He had spent years renting apartments, dealing with rising rent payments, noisy neighbors, and the frustration of feeling like his money disappeared every month without building any long-term value. Owning a home felt like a major milestone and proof that his sacrifices had finally paid off.

But within six months of closing on the property, reality began hitting harder than he expected. The mortgage payment was much larger than he originally imagined. After including property taxes, homeowner's insurance, utilities, maintenance, and unexpected repairs, his monthly housing costs consumed nearly sixty percent of his take-home income. Every month felt tight. He stopped going out with friends as often, delayed vacations, avoided unnecessary purchases, and constantly worried about unexpected bills. Even though he technically owned a home, he felt financially trapped.

One evening, while reviewing his bank account after paying his mortgage, Daniel realized he had less than four hundred dollars remaining for the rest of the month. He sat quietly at the kitchen table staring at his finances while feeling a growing sense of frustration. He had done everything society told him to do. He worked full-time, saved responsibly, maintained decent credit, and bought a modest property. Yet instead of feeling financially secure, he felt overwhelmed.

A few weeks later, Daniel met his friend Marcus for coffee. Marcus had always seemed financially relaxed despite earning a similar salary. During their conversation, Daniel mentioned how difficult homeownership had become.

"I thought buying a house would make life easier," Daniel admitted. "Instead, I feel broke all the time."

Marcus smiled. "You bought the wrong kind of property."

Daniel laughed. "What does that even mean?"

"You bought a house that only costs you money," Marcus replied. "You need a property that pays you back."

Marcus explained how he had purchased a duplex two years earlier. He lived in one unit while renting the other. The tenant's rent covered nearly seventy percent of his total mortgage payment. Because his housing costs were so low, Marcus aggressively paid down debt, invested extra money, and built savings rapidly.

Daniel listened carefully. He had never seriously considered real estate investing because he assumed investors needed huge amounts of money or dozens of properties. But Marcus explained that house hacking allowed ordinary people to use owner-occupied financing to purchase small multifamily properties with relatively low down payments.

For weeks afterward, Daniel could not stop thinking about the conversation.

Eventually, he began researching duplexes in nearby neighborhoods. At first, the numbers seemed impossible. But as he studied more properties, he realized something important. In many cases, the rental income from one unit could cover a significant portion of the mortgage payment. Some properties even generated enough rental income to cover nearly the entire mortgage. Daniel started running calculations every night after work. He compared his current single-family home expenses with potential duplex scenarios. The difference shocked him.

Six months later, Daniel made one of the most important decisions of his life. He sold his single-family home and purchased a duplex using an owner-occupied loan. The property was not glamorous. It needed cosmetic updates, fresh paint, and some repairs. But the numbers worked.

After moving into one side of the duplex, Daniel rented the second unit to a young couple. The rental income immediately covered over half of his mortgage payment. Suddenly, the financial pressure that had dominated his life began easing.

For the first time in years, Daniel could breathe.

Instead of barely surviving every month, he started saving aggressively. He created an emergency fund. He paid down credit card debt. He made extra principal payments toward the mortgage. The stress that once kept him awake at night slowly disappeared.

A year later, Daniel decided to take things further. He converted part of the garage into a small studio-style rental space after verifying local zoning rules and obtaining proper permits. The additional rental income created even more financial flexibility. By the third year, Daniel's mortgage balance had dropped far faster than expected. Between tenant payments, extra principal contributions, and rising property values, his equity position improved dramatically. Meanwhile, rents in the area continued increasing.

One night, Daniel sat on the back patio reviewing his finances again, but this time the feeling was completely different from the night he sat terrified at his kitchen table years earlier. Instead of panic, he felt peace.

The duplex had changed his entire financial future.

His housing costs were manageable. His savings were growing. His investments were increasing. Most importantly, he no longer felt trapped by his mortgage.

Eventually, Daniel purchased another small multifamily property while keeping the duplex as a long-term rental. The cash flow from both properties accelerated his wealth even further. Within ten years, he had built enough passive income to leave the corporate job he once feared losing.

Looking back, Daniel realized the biggest transformation had not been financial alone. It had been mental. He stopped viewing his home as a burden and began viewing real estate as a tool. That single shift changed everything. What started with one duplex and one tenant eventually created complete financial flexibility, long-term wealth, and the freedom to design life on his own terms.

Chapter 2

Choosing the Right Property for House Hacking and Mortgage Payoff Success

One of the most important decisions in any house hacking strategy is selecting the right property. A successful house hack begins long before the first tenant moves in or the first rental payment is collected. It begins during the property selection process itself. The type of property you purchase, the location you choose, the financing structure you use, and the income potential of the property will all directly impact how quickly you can reduce or eliminate your mortgage. Many people fail with real estate not because real estate itself is flawed, but because they purchase properties emotionally instead of strategically. They buy homes based entirely on appearance, status, or personal preference without considering the financial performance of the property. A house hacking property must be evaluated differently. It must function not only as a home but also as an income-producing asset capable of accelerating long-term financial growth.

The first step in selecting the right property is understanding your primary objective. In this series, the focus is mortgage payoff acceleration and long-term financial freedom. That means the ideal property is one capable of generating consistent rental income while maintaining manageable expenses. The stronger the cash flow, the faster the mortgage can potentially be reduced. Every dollar of rental income that offsets housing costs creates additional financial flexibility and increases the homeowner's ability to make extra principal payments or invest in additional opportunities.

Many first-time house hackers begin by considering small multifamily properties such as duplexes, triplexes, or fourplexes. These properties are often ideal because they allow the homeowner to live in one unit while renting out the others. In many cases, the rental income from the additional units covers a significant portion—or even all—of the mortgage payment. This strategy provides a major financial advantage because owner-occupied financing usually offers lower down payment requirements and lower interest rates than traditional investment property loans. A buyer who may not yet qualify for a large investment portfolio can still enter the real estate market strategically with one owner-occupied multifamily property.

A duplex is often considered one of the best starting points for new real estate investors because it balances simplicity with strong income potential. Living in one unit while renting the other provides both privacy and cash flow. The homeowner still enjoys the experience of living in a separate space while benefiting from tenant income. Triplexes and fourplexes can generate even stronger cash flow, although they may require more management and larger reserves. The key is evaluating how much rental income each property can realistically generate compared to the total monthly expenses.

Single-family homes can also work extremely well for house hacking depending on the layout and location. Many homeowners successfully rent spare bedrooms, basement suites, garage apartments, detached guest houses, or accessory dwelling units. In high-demand rental areas, even one additional room can significantly reduce monthly housing expenses. College towns, major employment centers, tourist destinations, and growing suburban markets often create strong demand for affordable room rentals or shared housing arrangements.

Location plays a critical role in determining whether a property will succeed financially. A beautiful property in the wrong location may struggle to attract tenants or generate sufficient income. On the other hand, a modest property in a strong rental market may produce excellent long-term cash flow. Areas near hospitals, universities, military bases, downtown business districts, transportation hubs, beaches, entertainment districts, or growing job markets often create consistent rental demand. Understanding the economic drivers of a location helps homeowners identify areas where rental income is more likely to remain stable and increase over time.

One of the biggest mistakes buyers make is overestimating future rental income while underestimating expenses. Conservative financial analysis is essential. Before purchasing a property, homeowners should carefully calculate all expected monthly costs, including mortgage payments, property taxes, insurance, utilities, maintenance, repairs, vacancy reserves, property management costs if applicable, homeowner association fees, landscaping, internet, and other recurring expenses. Underestimating expenses can quickly create financial pressure even when rental income appears strong initially.

At the same time, rental income projections should remain realistic and based on actual market data. Reviewing comparable rental listings, speaking with local property managers, researching occupancy trends, and analyzing seasonal demand all help create more accurate income estimates. The goal is not to create unrealistic optimism but to build a sustainable long-term strategy capable of performing even during slower economic conditions.

Cash flow analysis is one of the most important skills a successful house hacker can develop. Positive cash flow occurs when rental income exceeds total property expenses. Strong positive cash flow creates flexibility, security, and opportunities for accelerated mortgage reduction. However, even properties with modest or break-even cash flow can become powerful wealth-building tools if they are located in appreciating markets and structured intelligently. Appreciation, tax advantages, principal reduction, and future rental increases can significantly improve long-term returns.

Another major consideration when selecting a property is financing. Mortgage terms dramatically affect affordability and long-term cash flow. Interest rates, down payment size, loan programs, mortgage insurance, and loan duration all impact the monthly payment structure. Many first-time house hackers use FHA loans because they allow lower down payments and more flexible qualification standards. VA loans can also provide excellent opportunities for eligible military borrowers because of low down payment requirements and competitive interest rates. Conventional owner-occupied loans often work well for buyers with stronger credit profiles and larger down payments.

The relationship between mortgage debt and rental income must remain balanced. Some buyers become overly aggressive by purchasing properties that stretch their finances too thin. Even if rental income eventually offsets expenses, unexpected vacancies, repairs, or tenant issues can create temporary financial pressure. Maintaining emergency reserves and purchasing properties within reasonable affordability ranges helps reduce risk significantly.

Property layout is another critical factor in successful house hacking. Functional separation between living spaces often improves tenant satisfaction and homeowner comfort. Separate entrances, private bathrooms, soundproofing, dedicated parking areas, and independent kitchens can make rental spaces more desirable and reduce conflicts. Even small modifications to improve privacy can dramatically improve the long-term success of a rental arrangement.

Short-term rental opportunities have also transformed the house hacking landscape. Homeowners in vacation markets or major cities may generate substantial income by renting rooms or separate spaces to travelers. However, short-term rentals require more active management, frequent cleaning, customer communication, and compliance with local regulations. Some homeowners associations and municipalities restrict short-term rentals entirely. Researching local laws before purchasing a property is essential to avoid legal and financial problems later.

Zoning and permit regulations should never be ignored. Many homeowners become excited about converting garages, basements, or detached buildings into rental units without fully understanding local requirements. Illegal or unpermitted rental units can create insurance problems, fines, liability exposure, and resale complications. Smart investors verify zoning, permitting, and occupancy regulations before purchasing or modifying properties.

Future scalability also matters when selecting a house hacking property. A property should ideally support not only current financial goals but also future opportunities. Some homeowners eventually move out and convert the entire property into a rental investment. Others use equity growth and increased cash flow to purchase additional properties. Choosing a property with strong long-term rental appeal creates more flexibility for future wealth-building strategies.

Appreciation potential is another important consideration. While cash flow is essential for mortgage payoff acceleration, appreciation helps build long-term equity and net worth. Markets with population growth, job expansion, infrastructure development, and strong housing demand often create favorable appreciation trends over time. A property that generates rental income while increasing in value can become an extremely powerful financial asset.

Many successful house hackers focus heavily on "livable investments." They understand that the property must support both financial performance and quality of life. If the homeowner becomes miserable because of poor layout, unsafe neighborhoods, constant tenant conflicts, or extreme inconvenience, the strategy becomes difficult to sustain long term. The ideal property balances cash flow with livability. House hacking should improve financial flexibility without completely sacrificing comfort or stability.

Risk management must also remain part of the property selection process. Real estate always carries risks, including vacancies, repairs, market fluctuations, legal disputes, tenant damage, interest rate changes, and economic downturns. Smart investors prepare for these realities by maintaining reserves, purchasing appropriate insurance, screening tenants carefully, and avoiding overly aggressive debt structures. Financial discipline often matters more than property size or income level.

One powerful aspect of house hacking is that it allows homeowners to learn real estate investing gradually. Instead of immediately managing large apartment complexes or major investment portfolios, homeowners gain hands-on experience with leasing, maintenance, budgeting, tenant communication, and property operations while still living on-site. This creates valuable education that can later support larger investment opportunities. The property selection process ultimately determines how effective the mortgage payoff strategy becomes over time. A poorly chosen property may create stress and financial pressure, while a strategically selected property can dramatically accelerate wealth creation and mortgage elimination. The goal is not simply owning real estate. The goal is owning real estate that actively supports financial freedom.

Every successful real estate investor eventually realizes that properties are not just buildings. They are financial systems. Each property either drains cash flow or generates it. Each property either creates stress or increases flexibility. House hacking works because it transforms the homeowner's relationship with housing expenses entirely. Instead of carrying the mortgage alone, the property begins sharing the financial burden through income generation.

When homeowners learn how to choose properties strategically, they stop viewing homeownership purely emotionally and begin approaching it intelligently. That shift in thinking often becomes the beginning of long-term financial transformation. The right property can reduce decades of financial pressure, create recurring cash flow, build equity rapidly, and open the door to future investment opportunities that once seemed impossible. Most importantly, selecting the right property creates momentum. Once rental income begins reducing the mortgage burden, homeowners gain confidence and financial flexibility. Extra money becomes available for principal reduction, savings, investing, or lifestyle improvements. The property begins working for the homeowner instead of the homeowner constantly struggling to support the property. That transition is where true financial acceleration begins.

The Small Fourplex That Built a Future

When Sofia first heard the term "house hacking," she almost ignored it completely. She was thirty-five years old, worked as a physical therapist, and had spent years saving money while renting a small apartment near the hospital where she worked. Like many people, she dreamed of owning a beautiful single-family home with a large kitchen, a spacious backyard, and complete privacy. But every time she reviewed home prices in her area, she became discouraged.

Mortgage payments had risen sharply because of higher interest rates and property values. Even though Sofia earned a respectable income, the monthly costs of owning a traditional home felt overwhelming. She worried constantly about becoming house poor.

One afternoon during lunch, a coworker named Angela mentioned that she had recently purchased a duplex. "You bought a duplex?" Sofia asked. "Don't you want more privacy?"

Angela laughed. "I thought I did. But honestly, having tenants cover most of my mortgage changed my entire financial life."

Angela explained how she lived in one side of the duplex while renting the other side to a young family. The rental income covered nearly seventy-five percent of her monthly mortgage payment. Because her living expenses were so low, she aggressively paid off student loans and built investments much faster than before.

That conversation stayed in Sofia's mind for weeks.

Eventually, she began researching small multifamily properties online. At first, she focused on duplexes, but inventory was limited in the neighborhoods she liked. Then one evening she found a small fourplex listed slightly outside the city center. The building was older but well maintained. Each unit was modest but functional. Most importantly, the numbers caught her attention immediately.

Three of the four units were already rented.

Sofia ran the calculations repeatedly. The combined rental income from the three occupied units would cover nearly all of the projected mortgage payment, taxes, and insurance. She would live in the fourth unit herself while allowing the tenants to support most of the property expenses. The idea felt both exciting and terrifying.

Her family thought she was crazy.

"You worked so hard to buy a home," her mother said. "Why would you want tenants living next to you?"

"You should buy a nice house for yourself," her brother added. "Not an apartment building."

But Sofia kept thinking about the math.

If she purchased a traditional home, nearly half of her income would disappear toward housing costs every month. But with the fourplex, she could dramatically reduce her expenses while building equity at the same time.

After weeks of hesitation, she made an offer.

The inspection revealed minor repairs, but overall the property was solid. She used an owner-occupied loan program and closed on the property two months later.

The first year was not perfect.

One tenant constantly complained about parking. Another unit needed plumbing repairs shortly after closing. Sofia spent weekends learning about maintenance, budgeting, leases, and tenant communication. Some nights she questioned whether she had made the right decision.

But financially, something incredible was happening.

For the first time in her adult life, Sofia was not overwhelmed by housing costs.

Because the tenants covered most of the property expenses, she suddenly had extra money every month. She increased her retirement contributions. She paid down her car loan aggressively. She built a six-month emergency fund. Most importantly, she started making additional principal payments toward the mortgage.

Within two years, the rents increased modestly as leases renewed. Meanwhile, her mortgage payment remained stable because she had locked in a fixed interest rate. The property began generating positive monthly cash flow beyond simply covering expenses.

Then the neighborhood started changing.

New restaurants opened nearby. A large medical office complex began construction a few blocks away. Property values increased steadily. Demand for rentals grew stronger each year.

By year four, Sofia refinanced the property into a lower interest rate, reducing her monthly expenses even further. She continued applying extra cash flow toward principal reduction while saving for another investment property.

One evening, Sofia sat in her small apartment unit reviewing her finances. She realized something shocking.

Her net worth had increased more in four years with the fourplex than during the previous decade combined.

The tenants had helped pay down the mortgage. Property appreciation had increased her equity dramatically. Rental income had improved her monthly cash flow. Most importantly, she no longer felt trapped financially.

Eventually, Sofia purchased a second small multifamily property while keeping the original fourplex as a long-term investment. Years later, the combined rental income from both properties exceeded her original employment income from the hospital.

Looking back, Sofia realized the biggest difference came from choosing the right property from the beginning. Instead of buying emotionally, she purchased strategically. That one decision changed the direction of her financial future completely.

The fourplex was never her “dream home” in the traditional sense. But it became something far more valuable.

It became the property that gave her freedom.

Chapter 3

Using Rental Cash Flow to Accelerate Mortgage Payoff

One of the most powerful financial shifts a homeowner can experience occurs when rental income begins actively reducing mortgage debt month after month. At that point, the property transforms from being merely a place to live into a financial engine capable of generating long-term wealth and freedom. While many homeowners spend thirty years making standard mortgage payments according to the bank's schedule, strategic homeowners learn how to use rental cash flow to dramatically shorten that timeline. The difference between these two approaches can represent hundreds of thousands of dollars in saved interest, increased equity, and accelerated financial independence.

Most traditional homeowners rely almost entirely on active employment income to cover mortgage payments. Their salary supports the debt, and any interruption to that salary can create financial pressure quickly. However, when rental cash flow enters the equation, the homeowner gains an additional source of financial support that changes the structure of the mortgage entirely. Instead of one person carrying the entire burden alone, tenants contribute to paying down the debt.

Over time, this creates a compounding effect that can dramatically accelerate mortgage payoff and wealth accumulation.

To fully understand the power of rental cash flow, homeowners must first understand how mortgage amortization works. During the early years of most mortgage loans, a large percentage of each payment goes toward interest rather than principal. This means homeowners often build equity slowly at first even though they make consistent monthly payments. Mortgage lenders structure loans this way intentionally because interest represents a major source of profit. Without additional principal payments, many homeowners spend decades paying enormous amounts of interest before finally owning the property outright.

Rental cash flow changes this equation because it creates opportunities to apply additional money toward principal reduction. Even relatively small extra payments can significantly reduce the total interest paid over the life of a mortgage. For example, a homeowner receiving an extra $1,000 per month from rental income may choose to apply most or all of that money directly toward the loan principal. Over several years, this strategy can eliminate large portions of the mortgage balance far earlier than the original loan schedule projected. The mathematics behind accelerated principal reduction are extremely powerful. Every extra dollar applied toward principal immediately reduces future interest calculations because interest is based on the remaining loan balance. As the balance declines faster, future payments contain a larger percentage of principal and less interest. This creates momentum that continues compounding over time. Homeowners who consistently apply rental cash flow toward mortgage reduction often discover that the loan balance begins shrinking much faster than expected.

One of the biggest advantages of using rental income for mortgage payoff is that the homeowner is not sacrificing their entire personal lifestyle to achieve financial progress. Many traditional mortgage payoff plans require extreme budgeting, constant sacrifice, or eliminating nearly all discretionary spending. While discipline remains important, rental income creates an additional income stream that supports the payoff strategy without relying solely on the homeowner's employment earnings. This often makes the strategy more sustainable over the long term.

For example, imagine a homeowner with a $400,000 mortgage at a fixed interest rate over thirty years. Under a standard payment schedule, the homeowner may pay hundreds of thousands of dollars in interest before the loan is fully repaid. However, if the homeowner generates an additional $2,000 per month from rental income and applies even part of that income toward principal reduction, the payoff timeline may shrink dramatically. Instead of thirty years, the mortgage might be eliminated in fifteen or twenty years depending on consistency and loan structure.

Consistency is one of the most important factors in successful mortgage acceleration. Some homeowners receive rental income but spend it immediately on lifestyle upgrades, luxury purchases, vacations, or unnecessary expenses. While enjoying some benefits of increased cash flow is reasonable, the homeowners who achieve the greatest long-term financial success are often those who remain disciplined during the early years of wealth building. They prioritize debt reduction, reserve building, and investment growth before dramatically increasing lifestyle expenses.

Emergency reserves also remain essential when using rental income to accelerate mortgage payoff. Real estate investing always carries risks, including vacancies, repairs, economic downturns, tenant issues, or unexpected maintenance costs. Homeowners should avoid directing every dollar toward mortgage reduction while ignoring liquidity. A strong emergency fund provides stability during periods of uncertainty and prevents financial setbacks from turning into crises. Vacancies represent one of the most common realities of rental property ownership. Even excellent properties occasionally experience turnover periods between tenants. Smart homeowners plan for this possibility by maintaining reserve funds and avoiding overdependence on maximum occupancy assumptions. A financially stable house hacking strategy should still remain manageable even during temporary vacancies or reduced rental income periods.

Maintenance and repairs also play a major role in long-term rental property performance. Every property eventually requires upkeep, including roofing, plumbing, appliances, HVAC systems, flooring, painting, landscaping, and general repairs. Successful homeowners budget proactively for these expenses rather than reacting emotionally when problems arise. Rental income should support both mortgage acceleration and property preservation because maintaining property quality helps protect long-term rental demand and appreciation potential.

One powerful strategy many homeowners use is separating rental income from personal spending entirely. Instead of mixing all income into one general account, they create dedicated systems for managing rental cash flow. A portion may go toward reserves, another portion toward maintenance, and another portion directly toward extra principal payments. This structure creates discipline and prevents the homeowner from unintentionally wasting cash flow that could otherwise accelerate financial progress significantly.

Another important concept is understanding the balance between mortgage payoff and additional investing. Some homeowners aggressively focus on eliminating their mortgage first before pursuing additional investments. Others balance mortgage reduction with acquiring additional cash-flowing properties or investments. There is no universal answer because each strategy depends on risk tolerance, interest rates, market conditions, age, income stability, and long-term financial goals. However, regardless of the chosen balance, rental income provides flexibility and opportunities that traditional homeowners often lack.

As rental income increases over time, mortgage acceleration can become even more effective. In many markets, rents gradually rise due to inflation, population growth, and housing demand. Meanwhile, homeowners with fixed-rate mortgages often maintain relatively stable principal and interest payments. This creates expanding cash flow margins over time. A property that initially only slightly reduced housing expenses may eventually generate significant positive cash flow years later.

This is one reason real estate remains such a powerful long-term wealth-building tool. Inflation that negatively affects many expenses can actually benefit property owners with fixed-rate debt and increasing rental income. As rents rise, additional cash flow can be directed toward faster principal reduction, additional investments, or financial independence goals.

House hackers also benefit psychologically from seeing tangible financial progress. Many traditional homeowners feel discouraged because mortgage balances decline slowly during the early years of repayment. Rental income changes that experience. When homeowners see the balance shrinking faster because tenants are indirectly helping pay down the debt, motivation often increases dramatically. Financial progress becomes visible and measurable.

Some homeowners eventually reach a stage where rental income fully covers the mortgage payment and additional principal reduction simultaneously. At that point, the homeowner may effectively live for free while aggressively building equity. This creates extraordinary financial flexibility. Income previously consumed by housing expenses can now be redirected toward retirement accounts, business opportunities, travel, education, or additional real estate acquisitions.

Another advantage of using rental cash flow for mortgage acceleration is risk reduction over time. As the mortgage balance declines, the homeowner's financial vulnerability decreases significantly. Lower debt obligations create greater stability during economic downturns or personal income disruptions. A homeowner with a nearly paid-off property experiences far less financial pressure than someone carrying maximum long-term debt with no additional income streams.

The concept of "financial breathing room" becomes increasingly important throughout this journey. Many people underestimate the emotional freedom that comes from reducing mortgage debt aggressively. Lower housing expenses improve mental clarity, reduce stress, increase confidence, and create opportunities that may have once seemed unrealistic. Entrepreneurship, career transitions, early retirement, or lifestyle changes become much more attainable when mortgage obligations shrink substantially.

Technology has also made managing rental cash flow easier than ever before. Homeowners can now automate rent collection, track expenses digitally, analyze cash flow performance, communicate with tenants online, and monitor financial progress efficiently. These tools help simplify operations and reduce many of the traditional frustrations associated with property management.

Tax advantages may further improve the effectiveness of rental cash flow strategies. Depending on local laws and individual circumstances, homeowners may benefit from deductions related to mortgage interest, depreciation, maintenance expenses, utilities, insurance, repairs, and other property-related costs. Working with knowledgeable tax professionals can help maximize these benefits while maintaining compliance with regulations.

Long-term wealth creation ultimately depends on how effectively homeowners manage cash flow. Many high-income individuals remain financially stressed because they spend nearly everything they earn. Meanwhile, moderate-income homeowners who strategically use rental income often achieve financial independence much faster because they understand leverage, cash flow management, and debt reduction principles.

The key lesson is simple yet profound: rental cash flow can dramatically accelerate mortgage payoff when used intentionally and consistently. The property itself begins contributing to its own debt elimination. Instead of depending entirely on personal labor income, the homeowner leverages real estate income to create financial momentum. Over time, this strategy transforms not only the mortgage balance but also the homeowner's overall financial future.

A mortgage does not need to remain a thirty-year burden. With intelligent rental strategies, disciplined cash flow management, and consistent principal reduction, homeowners can shorten that timeline dramatically while building equity, increasing financial flexibility, and creating lasting wealth. Rental income becomes more than extra money. It becomes a powerful tool capable of accelerating freedom itself.

The Basement Apartment Strategy

When Melissa purchased her home at age thirty-eight, she believed she had finally found stability after years of financial struggle. As a single mother raising two children, she spent most of her adult life working multiple jobs while renting small apartments that constantly increased in price. Owning a home represented security, pride, and a better future for her family.

At first, everything felt exciting.

The house was modest but beautiful to her. It had a small backyard, three bedrooms, and a finished basement. Melissa imagined family dinners, birthdays, holiday gatherings, and finally having a place her children could truly call home.

But within the first year, the financial pressure became intense.

Between the mortgage payment, property taxes, utilities, insurance, groceries, school expenses, and maintenance costs, nearly every paycheck disappeared immediately. Even small unexpected repairs created panic. One broken water heater forced Melissa to use credit cards because her savings account was nearly empty.

Late one night after putting her children to bed, Melissa sat at the kitchen table staring at unpaid bills. Exhaustion covered her face. She realized she could not continue living under constant financial stress for the next thirty years.

The next morning, while speaking with a coworker at the medical office where she worked, Melissa casually mentioned her financial frustrations.

"Do you use your basement?" her coworker asked.

"Not really," Melissa replied. "It's mostly storage and an old couch."

"You should rent it out."

Melissa immediately rejected the idea.

"I can't have strangers living in my house," she said.

But the idea stayed in her mind for weeks.

Eventually, she started researching basement apartment conversions online. She discovered that many homeowners legally converted basements into rental units with separate entrances, small kitchens, and private bathrooms. In her area, rental demand was extremely strong because housing costs had risen rapidly near the city.

After carefully reviewing local zoning requirements and speaking with contractors, Melissa realized the conversion was possible.

The process was not easy.

She spent several months saving money, completing repairs gradually, and improving the basement space. She installed durable flooring, added a small kitchenette, upgraded lighting, painted the walls, and created a private entrance from the side of the house.

When the apartment was finally ready, Melissa listed it online nervously.

Within forty-eight hours, she received dozens of inquiries.

Eventually, she rented the basement apartment to a quiet graduate student named Emily who worked nearby and needed affordable housing close to campus.

The rental income changed Melissa's life almost immediately.

For the first time since purchasing the home, she could comfortably pay the mortgage without fear. Instead of barely surviving every month, she finally had breathing room. She built an emergency fund. She stopped relying on credit cards. She even began making small extra payments toward the mortgage principal.

Over time, Melissa became more disciplined with the rental income. Instead of treating it like spending money, she used it strategically. Part of the rent went toward reserves for repairs and maintenance. Another portion went directly toward reducing the mortgage balance.

Year after year, the mortgage principal declined faster.

Meanwhile, property values in the neighborhood increased steadily. The basement apartment continued generating consistent income because rental demand remained strong.

Five years later, Melissa refinanced the mortgage into a lower interest rate while keeping the same aggressive payoff strategy. The lower payment allowed her to direct even more money toward principal reduction.

Her children noticed the difference too.

Their mother smiled more often. Financial stress no longer dominated every conversation. Vacations became possible again. College savings accounts slowly began growing. The atmosphere inside the home completely changed. One evening, Melissa reviewed her mortgage balance online and realized she had reduced the loan far faster than she ever thought possible. What once seemed like an impossible thirty-year burden suddenly looked manageable.

The basement apartment had become more than a rental space.

It became the financial turning point that transformed her family's future.

Years later, Melissa often shared her story with friends struggling financially. Many of them assumed real estate investing required massive wealth or multiple properties. Melissa would simply smile and tell them the truth.

"It started with one unused basement and one decision," she would say.

That one decision eventually created stability, confidence, growing equity, reduced debt, and long-term financial freedom for her entire family.

Chapter 4

Creating a Mortgage Payoff System Using Rental Income and Financial Discipline

One of the biggest mistakes homeowners make when receiving rental income is failing to create a structured system for using that income strategically. Many people begin house hacking or renting portions of their property successfully, but instead of accelerating financial progress, they gradually absorb the additional cash flow into lifestyle inflation. They buy newer cars, increase discretionary spending, upgrade vacations, or spend the extra money without a long-term plan. While enjoying some benefits of increased cash flow is understandable, homeowners who create lasting wealth usually follow disciplined financial systems that direct rental income intentionally toward mortgage reduction, reserves, investments, and long-term financial goals.

The purpose of this chapter is to show how rental income alone does not automatically create financial freedom. What creates freedom is the system used to manage that income consistently over time. A well-designed mortgage payoff system transforms rental cash flow into a powerful financial engine capable of eliminating debt years earlier while simultaneously building security and long-term wealth.

The first principle of building a mortgage payoff system is separating emotion from financial management. Many homeowners operate financially based on feelings instead of strategy. When money enters the account, they spend impulsively without evaluating long-term consequences. Successful homeowners take a different approach. They create automated financial structures that prioritize debt reduction and wealth building before discretionary spending occurs.

One of the simplest and most effective systems involves dividing rental income into predetermined categories immediately after receiving it. Instead of treating all rental income as personal spending money, the homeowner allocates percentages toward specific financial objectives. For example, one portion may go toward maintenance reserves, another toward emergency savings, another toward taxes if necessary, and another directly toward additional mortgage principal payments.

This structure creates consistency and prevents financial drift. Over time, small disciplined decisions compound into extraordinary results. Many homeowners underestimate how dramatically regular extra mortgage payments can reduce interest expenses and shorten loan timelines. Automation also plays a major role in successful mortgage payoff systems. When homeowners rely entirely on motivation or memory to make extra payments, inconsistency often develops. Life becomes busy, expenses arise, and financial goals lose momentum. Automated systems reduce this problem significantly. Setting up recurring additional principal payments creates discipline without requiring constant decision-making.

For example, a homeowner receiving consistent rental income every month may establish an automatic extra principal payment immediately after rent collection occurs. Instead of waiting to see what money remains at the end of the month, the system prioritizes mortgage reduction first. This approach treats accelerated payoff as a fixed financial priority rather than an optional leftover decision.

Another critical element of a successful payoff system is maintaining financial reserves. Many homeowners become excited about eliminating their mortgage quickly and direct every available dollar toward principal reduction. While aggressive debt reduction can be powerful, eliminating liquidity entirely creates unnecessary risk. Rental properties inevitably experience vacancies, repairs, maintenance issues, and economic fluctuations. Without adequate reserves, even small financial setbacks can force homeowners back into credit card debt or personal loans. Emergency reserves create stability and confidence. Homeowners should ideally maintain reserves covering several months of mortgage payments, property expenses, and personal living costs. This cushion allows the homeowner to continue operating strategically during temporary disruptions without panicking or abandoning long-term financial goals.

Maintenance reserves are equally important. Every property eventually requires repairs and updates. Roofs wear out. HVAC systems fail. Plumbing leaks occur. Appliances break. Flooring deteriorates. Ignoring maintenance planning often leads homeowners into financial stress later. Smart investors treat maintenance as a predictable business expense rather than an unexpected emergency.

One common strategy involves allocating a percentage of rental income specifically toward future repairs and capital expenditures. This reserve account gradually grows over time and reduces the financial impact of larger maintenance projects. Properties that remain well maintained also tend to attract higher-quality tenants, maintain stronger occupancy rates, and preserve long-term appreciation potential.

Another powerful principle in mortgage payoff systems is increasing principal payments as rental income grows. Many markets experience gradual rent increases over time due to inflation, population growth, housing shortages, or local economic development. Meanwhile, homeowners with fixed-rate mortgages maintain relatively stable mortgage payments. This creates expanding cash flow margins as rental income rises.

Instead of absorbing these increases into lifestyle spending, disciplined homeowners redirect the additional cash flow toward mortgage acceleration. Over several years, even moderate rental increases can dramatically increase the speed of principal reduction.

For example, a homeowner who initially receives $1,500 monthly rental income may eventually receive $2,000 or more as rents rise. If the mortgage payment remains relatively stable, the additional cash flow creates increasing opportunities for accelerated debt elimination. This compounding effect becomes one of the most powerful aspects of long-term real estate ownership.

Tracking progress is another important part of maintaining motivation and financial discipline. Mortgage balances often feel overwhelming when viewed as large long-term obligations.

However, consistent progress tracking helps homeowners visualize momentum. Watching the principal balance decline faster than scheduled creates psychological reinforcement that encourages continued discipline.

Some homeowners create mortgage payoff charts, spreadsheets, or dashboards showing projected payoff dates under different extra payment scenarios. Others celebrate financial milestones such as eliminating five years from the mortgage term or reducing the balance below major thresholds. These visual indicators transform mortgage reduction from an abstract goal into measurable progress.

Mindset also matters tremendously. Many people view mortgage debt as permanent or unavoidable. They accept thirty-year repayment timelines as normal because most society operates that way. However, homeowners who successfully eliminate mortgages early usually develop a completely different mindset about debt and cash flow. They see rental income as leverage capable of accelerating freedom rather than simply supplementing lifestyle spending.

Another important concept involves balancing mortgage payoff with other financial objectives. Some homeowners become so focused on eliminating debt that they neglect retirement investing, business opportunities, or liquidity entirely. Others ignore debt reduction completely while overextending themselves with additional investments. Sustainable wealth building usually requires balance. The ideal mortgage payoff system aligns with the homeowner's overall financial goals, age, risk tolerance, market conditions, and lifestyle preferences. Someone nearing retirement may prioritize aggressive debt elimination for security and peace of mind. A younger investor with strong cash flow and low-interest debt may balance mortgage reduction with acquiring additional cash-flowing properties. The strategy must remain personalized and adaptable.

Taxes also influence mortgage payoff decisions. Depending on the homeowner's situation, mortgage interest deductions, depreciation, business expenses, and rental property tax treatment may affect overall financial planning. Consulting qualified tax professionals can help homeowners optimize their strategy while remaining compliant with regulations.

Lifestyle inflation represents one of the greatest threats to long-term mortgage payoff success. As rental income increases, many homeowners unconsciously increase spending simultaneously. New subscriptions, luxury purchases, expensive vehicles, dining habits, and lifestyle upgrades gradually consume the financial advantages rental income originally created. Preventing this pattern requires intentional discipline and clarity about long-term goals. Financial freedom often depends less on income level and more on cash flow management. Some people earning extremely high incomes remain financially stressed because expenses consume everything they earn. Meanwhile, moderate-income homeowners who manage rental income intelligently often achieve extraordinary financial flexibility because they prioritize debt reduction and wealth creation consistently.

The emotional benefits of mortgage reduction should also not be underestimated. As the mortgage balance declines, homeowners often experience increasing confidence, reduced stress, improved relationships, and greater career flexibility. Lower debt obligations reduce vulnerability during economic downturns and create options that may have once seemed impossible.

Many homeowners pursuing aggressive mortgage payoff strategies eventually reach a stage where rental income covers most or all housing expenses while simultaneously reducing the loan balance. At that point, financial momentum accelerates dramatically. Employment income can increasingly support investments, retirement accounts, business opportunities, or personal freedom rather than merely surviving monthly obligations.

Long-term consistency ultimately matters more than short-term intensity. Some homeowners attempt extreme financial sacrifices for brief periods but eventually burn out. Sustainable systems create lasting success because they can be maintained year after year. Even moderate additional principal payments consistently applied over long periods create enormous results due to compounding interest savings.

A mortgage payoff system is not merely about numbers. It is about creating structure, discipline, and intentionality around financial decisions. Rental income provides the opportunity, but systems create the results. Homeowners who combine cash-flowing real estate with disciplined financial management often achieve levels of stability and freedom far beyond what traditional income alone could provide.

Most importantly, homeowners must remember that every extra principal payment permanently changes the future. Every dollar reducing mortgage debt eliminates future interest obligations and increases ownership equity. Over time, those consistent decisions gradually transform the homeowner from someone burdened by debt into someone building long-term financial independence.

The property itself becomes a financial partner in the journey toward freedom. Instead of consuming endless income for decades, it actively contributes to eliminating its own debt. That transformation is where real financial acceleration begins.

How Rental Income Can Cut a 30-Year Mortgage Nearly in Half

This example shows how house hacking can dramatically speed up mortgage payoff. A homeowner buys a duplex for $500,000 with a 10% down payment and a $450,000 mortgage at 6.5% interest. The monthly mortgage payment is about $2,844, and after adding taxes and insurance, total housing costs are about $3,644 per month.

The homeowner rents out the second unit for $2,200 per month. This reduces their real housing cost to about $1,444 per month, since the tenant is covering a large portion of the mortgage and expenses. This makes the property much more affordable than a traditional home where the owner pays everything alone.

If the homeowner only makes the standard payments, the mortgage takes 30 years to pay off and costs about $1,023,840 total, including roughly $573,840 in interest. This means over half a million dollars is paid in interest alone over the life of the loan.

However, in the accelerated strategy, the homeowner uses

rental income and savings to add an extra $1,500 per month toward the mortgage. This increases the total monthly payment to about $4,344 and shortens the payoff timeline to around 13 years and 8 months instead of 30 years.

Because of this aggressive but structured approach, the homeowner saves about $336,840 in interest over time. On top of that, the property likely appreciates in value, potentially reaching around $854,000 after 14 years, while the mortgage balance is eliminated much earlier than normal.

The key lesson is that house hacking turns a property from a simple expense into a wealth-building tool. By using rental income to reduce costs and accelerate debt payoff, homeowners can build equity faster, save hundreds of thousands in interest, and reach financial freedom years earlier than with a traditional mortgage approach.

Chapter 5

Scaling Beyond One Property – Using House Hacking to Build Long-Term Wealth and Mortgage Freedom

One of the most powerful realizations many homeowners experience after successfully house hacking their first property is that the strategy can extend far beyond reducing a single mortgage payment. What begins as a method for lowering housing costs often evolves into a long-term wealth-building system capable of creating multiple income streams, substantial equity growth, and complete financial transformation. The first property teaches financial discipline, cash flow management, tenant relations, financing strategies, and real estate operations. Once homeowners gain confidence and experience, they begin understanding that one successful property can eventually lead to an entire portfolio of income-producing assets.

Many financially successful real estate investors started with a single house hack. They did not begin with massive wealth, large apartment complexes, or institutional investors backing them. Instead, they started with one strategically chosen property that reduced their living expenses and increased financial flexibility. Over time, the cash flow, equity growth, and knowledge generated from that property created opportunities to acquire additional investments. This process of gradual scaling becomes one of the most effective paths toward long-term mortgage freedom and financial independence.

The first major advantage of scaling beyond one property is diversification of income streams. A homeowner relying solely on one salary remains vulnerable to job loss, economic downturns, industry disruptions, or unexpected emergencies. Rental properties create additional sources of income that reduce dependence on active employment. As multiple properties generate cash flow simultaneously, financial stability often increases dramatically.

For example, a homeowner who initially reduces housing costs through house hacking may later use savings and equity growth to purchase a second property. The first property may continue generating rental income while the homeowner either moves into the second property or operates both as investments. Over time, the combined cash flow from multiple properties can exceed the homeowner's original salary. At that point, the relationship between work, debt, and financial security changes entirely. Equity growth plays a major role in scaling strategies. As mortgage balances decline and property values increase, homeowners build equity that can later support additional investments. Equity represents one of the most powerful wealth-building tools in real estate because it creates leverage opportunities unavailable to many traditional savers or investors. A homeowner who builds substantial equity in one property may eventually use refinancing, home equity lines of credit, or strategic property sales to acquire additional cash-flowing assets.

However, scaling must be approached intelligently and cautiously. One of the biggest mistakes inexperienced investors make is becoming overly aggressive too quickly. Excitement from initial success can lead homeowners to overextend financially, purchase poor-quality properties, ignore reserves, or assume appreciation and rental growth will always continue smoothly. Sustainable wealth building requires patience, discipline, and strong risk management.

Cash flow should remain the foundation of every scaling decision. Many investors focus excessively on appreciation while ignoring monthly profitability. While appreciation can create substantial long-term wealth, properties that consistently lose money every month create stress and financial instability. Positive cash flow provides the stability necessary to survive market fluctuations, vacancies, repairs, and economic uncertainty. The concept of "snowballing" rental income becomes increasingly important during portfolio growth. As one property generates additional cash flow, that income can help fund reserves, down payments, or accelerated debt reduction on future properties. Each successful property strengthens the overall financial system. Over time, multiple properties create compounding effects through appreciation, mortgage reduction, tax advantages, and rising rental income.

One major strategic decision homeowners face when scaling is whether to aggressively pay off existing mortgages first or acquire additional properties more quickly. Some investors prioritize eliminating debt for security and peace of mind before expanding aggressively. Others leverage low-interest debt to acquire additional income-producing properties sooner. Both approaches can succeed depending on the investor's personality, goals, market conditions, age, and risk tolerance.

For conservative investors, paying down debt aggressively may provide emotional stability and lower long-term risk exposure. Lower debt obligations reduce vulnerability during recessions, vacancies, or economic disruptions. Meanwhile, more growth-oriented investors may prefer using available capital to purchase additional properties while maintaining manageable leverage. There is no universal answer. The correct approach depends on balancing opportunity with sustainability. Another critical factor in scaling successfully is operational efficiency. Managing one property differs significantly from managing several properties. Systems become increasingly important as portfolios grow. Rent collection, maintenance coordination, bookkeeping, tenant communication, lease management, insurance tracking, tax preparation, and legal compliance all become more complex with additional units.

Technology can significantly simplify these responsibilities. Modern property management software allows landlords to automate rent collection, track expenses, manage leases, communicate with tenants, monitor vacancies, and analyze cash flow efficiently. Systems reduce stress and allow investors to focus on long-term strategy rather than daily chaos.

Financing strategies also evolve as investors scale. The first property often uses owner-occupied financing because it offers favorable terms and lower down payment requirements. Future properties may involve conventional investment loans, portfolio loans, DSCR loans, commercial financing, seller financing, partnerships, or creative financing strategies depending on the investor's goals and experience level.

Credit management becomes increasingly important during expansion. Mortgage lenders evaluate debt-to-income ratios, credit scores, reserve levels, rental income history, and cash flow strength when approving additional loans. Investors who maintain strong financial discipline usually gain greater access to financing opportunities over time.

Location selection remains equally important during scaling. Some investors prefer concentrating properties within the same geographic area to simplify management and market expertise. Others diversify across different cities or states to reduce local market risk. Each approach has advantages and disadvantages. Concentrated portfolios may allow stronger operational efficiency, while geographic diversification may reduce exposure to localized economic downturns.

Appreciation and cash flow markets also differ significantly. Some areas offer strong monthly cash flow but slower appreciation. Others provide substantial appreciation potential with lower immediate cash flow. Successful investors often balance these factors carefully based on long-term objectives.

One of the greatest long-term benefits of scaling beyond one property is the increasing separation between personal labor income and financial survival. Many people spend decades trapped in cycles where employment income barely covers living expenses. Rental properties gradually shift that dynamic by creating recurring income streams independent of direct labor hours. As mortgage balances decline and cash flow grows, homeowners often gain increasing control over their time, career choices, and lifestyle decisions. The emotional transformation can be just as powerful as the financial transformation. Financial stress decreases significantly when housing expenses are supported by rental income. Confidence increases. Long-term planning becomes easier. Homeowners begin making decisions from positions of strength rather than survival.

Another major advantage of scaling strategically is inflation protection. Fixed-rate mortgage debt often becomes easier to manage over time as rents and property values increase. Meanwhile, rental income may continue rising while loan payments remain relatively stable. This expanding cash flow margin creates additional opportunities for accelerated debt reduction and investment growth.

However, scaling also requires emotional resilience. Real estate investing is not always smooth or predictable. Vacancies occur. Repairs happen unexpectedly. Markets fluctuate. Tenants sometimes create challenges. Economic conditions change. Successful investors develop the ability to remain calm, disciplined, and solutions-focused during setbacks.

Education and networking also become increasingly valuable as portfolios grow. Many successful investors continuously study financing, tax strategies, property management, negotiation, construction, market analysis, and legal considerations. Relationships with lenders, contractors, accountants, attorneys, insurance agents, and experienced investors often create opportunities and prevent costly mistakes.

Lifestyle design should remain part of the scaling process as well. Some investors aggressively pursue maximum growth at the expense of personal balance, relationships, or health. Others intentionally build portfolios that support flexibility, family time, travel, or early retirement goals. Wealth building should ultimately support quality of life rather than create constant burnout and stress.

One important lesson many investors eventually learn is that freedom often comes from cash flow rather than property count alone. Owning many properties with excessive debt and poor cash flow may create more stress than freedom. By contrast, a smaller portfolio of well-managed, profitable properties with reasonable leverage can provide tremendous financial stability and lifestyle flexibility.

House hacking provides one of the most accessible starting points for this journey because it lowers the barrier to entry into real estate ownership and investment. Instead of waiting decades to accumulate wealth slowly through savings alone, homeowners begin leveraging real estate cash flow much earlier in life. Over time, the compounding effects become enormous.

A homeowner who successfully scales beyond one property often reaches a point where rental income covers not only housing expenses but also major portions of overall living expenses. At that stage, mortgage freedom becomes increasingly achievable. Additional properties may continue generating income long after mortgages are eliminated entirely, creating true long-term wealth and financial independence.

The process rarely happens overnight. Most successful real estate investors build portfolios gradually over many years through discipline, patience, education, and consistent decision-making. But each property builds upon the last. Each mortgage reduction increases equity. Each successful tenant relationship improves experience. Each additional cash flow stream strengthens overall financial security.

Ultimately, scaling beyond one property transforms house hacking from a temporary financial tactic into a complete long-term wealth strategy. The homeowner evolves from simply reducing housing costs into building a financial system where real estate income actively supports freedom, security, opportunity, and long-term independence.

The journey often begins with one property, one tenant, and one decision to think differently about housing. But over time, that single decision can create a future entirely different from the traditional path of decades of debt and financial pressure.

Building a Small Real Estate Portfolio Through House Hacking

This example shows how a homeowner can start with one smart property purchase and eventually build multiple income-producing properties. The first property is a duplex purchased for $450,000 using a small 5% down payment. The monthly cost of owning the property is about $3,312, but one unit is rented out for $2,100 per month, which significantly reduces the homeowner's personal housing expense.

After rental income, the homeowner is only paying about $1,212 per month to live in the property. Instead of just saving that money, they decide to use an extra $1,000 per month to aggressively pay down the mortgage. This helps them reduce the loan payoff time from 30 years to about 16 years, while also saving around $240,000 in interest over the life of the loan.

As the property appreciates and the mortgage balance drops faster, the homeowner builds equity much quicker than normal. After about 5 years, the property is worth roughly $547,000, while the remaining mortgage is about $340,000. This gives them around $207,000 in equity, which can be used for future investing opportunities. With this equity and savings, the homeowner moves on to purchase a second property—a triplex for $600,000 with 20% down. This property generates about $5,400 in monthly rent and, after expenses, produces nearly $1,000 per month in positive cash flow. Now the homeowner owns two income-producing properties instead of just one.

Combined, both properties generate about $7,500 per month in rental income, while also reducing the owner's personal housing costs by over $2,000 per month. Together, this creates more than $3,000 per month in financial advantage compared to traditional homeownership, along with strong appreciation and tax benefits over time.

The key lesson is that house hacking is not just about lowering your own housing cost—it can be the starting point for building a full real estate portfolio. By using rental income, equity growth, and smart reinvestment strategies, a single property can turn into multiple assets that generate cash flow, build wealth, and move the homeowner closer to long-term financial freedom.

Chapter 6

Risk Management, Vacancies, and Protecting Your Mortgage Payoff Strategy

One of the most important realities every homeowner and real estate investor must understand is that no rental strategy is completely risk-free. While house hacking and rental income can dramatically accelerate mortgage payoff and long-term wealth creation, success depends heavily on preparation, discipline, and risk management. Many inexperienced investors focus only on the exciting side of real estate—the cash flow, appreciation, equity growth, and financial freedom—while ignoring the challenges that naturally come with property ownership. However, the homeowners who build lasting wealth are usually not the ones who avoid all problems entirely. They are the ones who prepare for problems before they occur and create systems capable of surviving temporary setbacks.

The truth is that every rental property will eventually experience vacancies, repairs, tenant turnover, maintenance expenses, economic fluctuations, or unexpected financial challenges. These situations are not signs of failure. They are normal parts of operating real estate over long periods of time. The key difference between financially stable investors and financially stressed investors is how they respond to these challenges. Strong risk management allows homeowners to continue progressing toward mortgage freedom even during difficult periods.

One of the biggest financial threats to any mortgage payoff strategy is vacancy. Vacancy occurs when rental space sits empty without generating income. During vacancy periods, the homeowner must still cover mortgage payments, property taxes, insurance, utilities, and maintenance expenses even though rental revenue has temporarily stopped. Investors who rely entirely on rental income without maintaining reserves often experience tremendous stress during these periods.

Vacancies can happen for many reasons. A tenant may relocate for work, purchase a home, experience financial hardship, or simply choose not to renew a lease. In short-term rentals, occupancy may decline during slower seasons or economic downturns. Local oversupply, poor property condition, increased competition, or changing neighborhood trends may also reduce rental demand temporarily.

The most effective way to manage vacancy risk is through preparation rather than reaction. Successful homeowners maintain vacancy reserves specifically designed to cover expenses during periods without tenants. Instead of assuming a property will remain occupied every day of the year, experienced investors build conservative financial projections that account for occasional downtime.

For example, many landlords estimate vacancy expenses by setting aside a percentage of monthly rental income every month. Over time, this reserve account grows and creates financial protection. When a vacancy eventually occurs, the homeowner can continue making mortgage payments without panic or financial desperation.

Emergency savings represent another essential component of risk management. Many homeowners become overly aggressive about paying off their mortgage and direct every available dollar toward principal reduction. While accelerated mortgage payoff is valuable, eliminating liquidity completely creates unnecessary vulnerability. Financial reserves provide flexibility and stability during unexpected situations such as major repairs, medical emergencies, job loss, or economic downturns.

Maintenance issues represent another unavoidable reality of property ownership. Every property deteriorates gradually over time and requires ongoing upkeep. Roofs eventually need replacement. Plumbing systems develop leaks. Air conditioning systems fail. Appliances break. Flooring wears down. Water damage occurs. Landscaping requires maintenance. Ignoring these realities can quickly destroy cash flow and create long-term financial damage.

One of the biggest mistakes inexperienced investors make is underestimating maintenance costs during property analysis. A property may appear highly profitable initially, but without realistic maintenance budgeting, long-term cash flow projections become misleading. Smart investors proactively allocate money toward future repairs instead of reacting emotionally when problems arise.

Preventive maintenance often saves substantial money over time. Small issues addressed early frequently prevent larger and more expensive repairs later. For example, a minor roof leak repaired immediately may cost a few hundred dollars. Ignoring the problem could eventually lead to major water damage costing thousands. Responsible property owners understand that maintenance is not an inconvenience–it is part of preserving the long-term value and profitability of the investment.

Tenant quality also plays a major role in risk management. Poor tenant selection can create enormous financial and emotional stress. Late payments, property damage, lease violations, illegal activity, neighbor complaints, or eviction proceedings can quickly turn profitable properties into financial burdens. Careful tenant screening dramatically reduces these risks.

Strong tenant screening usually includes verifying income, checking employment history, reviewing credit reports, contacting prior landlords, conducting background checks where legally permitted, and evaluating overall reliability. Many experienced landlords believe that selecting the right tenant is one of the most important decisions affecting long-term property success.

Clear lease agreements are equally important. A professionally written lease establishes expectations regarding rent payments, maintenance responsibilities, occupancy rules, pets, security deposits, utilities, late fees, and property usage. Clear communication reduces misunderstandings and provides legal protection when disputes arise.

Insurance protection is another critical component of protecting mortgage payoff strategies. Many homeowners mistakenly assume standard homeowner insurance automatically covers all rental situations. However, rental activity may require specialized landlord policies, short-term rental endorsements, umbrella liability coverage, or additional protection depending on how the property is used. Failing to disclose rental activity properly to insurance providers can create devastating consequences if claims are denied after accidents or property damage. Responsible investors regularly review insurance coverage to ensure adequate protection for both property and liability exposure.

Economic downturns also affect rental properties differently depending on location, property type, and rental strategy. During recessions, some rental markets remain relatively stable while others experience declining rents or increased vacancies. Homeowners who maintain conservative leverage, strong reserves, and stable cash flow generally navigate difficult periods far more successfully than those operating with minimal margins.

Interest rates can also impact long-term investment performance. Rising rates may reduce buyer demand, increase financing costs, or slow appreciation temporarily. Homeowners with fixed-rate mortgages usually maintain greater stability because their principal and interest payments remain predictable despite broader market changes.

Diversification becomes increasingly important as investors scale into multiple properties. Relying entirely on one tenant or one property creates concentrated risk exposure. Multiple income streams, different tenant types, or properties in different locations may help reduce overall portfolio volatility. However, diversification should occur thoughtfully rather than aggressively.

Another major risk factor involves overleveraging. Some investors become overly optimistic during strong markets and purchase properties with extremely thin cash flow margins or excessive debt obligations. While leverage can accelerate wealth building, excessive leverage magnifies risk significantly during downturns or vacancies. Sustainable investing prioritizes manageable debt levels and realistic cash flow projections.

Lifestyle management also matters more than many investors realize. Some homeowners become so focused on scaling rapidly or eliminating mortgages aggressively that they create constant financial pressure and emotional exhaustion. Burnout can lead to poor decisions, neglected maintenance, damaged relationships, or abandoning long-term strategies entirely. Sustainable financial success requires balancing ambition with stability and quality of life.

One overlooked aspect of risk management is maintaining strong relationships with contractors, lenders, accountants, insurance agents, and legal professionals. Reliable professionals help investors respond more effectively when challenges arise. Delays, poor repairs, financing issues, or legal misunderstandings often become far more costly without experienced support systems.

Technology has improved risk management significantly for modern property owners. Online rent collection systems, maintenance tracking platforms, accounting software, tenant screening services, smart home technology, and property monitoring tools all help reduce operational risk and improve efficiency. These systems provide better organization, communication, and financial visibility.

Mindset ultimately plays one of the largest roles in successful risk management. Many people panic during temporary setbacks because they view problems emotionally instead of strategically. Experienced investors understand that vacancies, repairs, and market fluctuations are normal business realities rather than catastrophic failures. Preparation creates confidence. Financial reserves create patience. Systems create stability.

Mortgage freedom is not achieved simply through optimism or aggressive payoff strategies alone. It is achieved through consistency, discipline, and the ability to survive inevitable challenges without abandoning the long-term plan. A homeowner who aggressively pays down debt but cannot survive one vacancy or repair emergency remains financially vulnerable despite strong intentions. The goal of risk management is not eliminating all uncertainty entirely. Real estate will always involve some level of unpredictability. Instead, the goal is creating financial systems strong enough to absorb temporary setbacks while continuing progressing toward long-term financial freedom.

Over time, homeowners who manage risk effectively gain increasing confidence and stability. Vacancies become manageable instead of terrifying. Repairs become planned expenses instead of financial disasters. Rental income becomes dependable support rather than fragile hope. The mortgage payoff strategy strengthens because it rests on solid financial foundations rather than unrealistic assumptions.

One of the greatest emotional benefits of strong risk management is peace of mind. Homeowners with reserves, systems, insurance protection, quality tenants, and conservative financial structures sleep differently than those constantly operating under financial pressure. They make decisions calmly, think long term, and continue building wealth steadily regardless of temporary challenges.

Ultimately, protecting your mortgage payoff strategy is just as important as creating it. Rental income and house hacking can absolutely transform financial futures, but sustainable success requires preparation, patience, and disciplined management. The homeowners who achieve long-term freedom are usually not the ones who avoid every problem. They are the ones who prepare intelligently, adapt consistently, and continue moving forward even when obstacles appear.

How Proper Risk Management Protects a House Hacking Strategy

This example shows how house hacking can work well, but also why having savings and planning for risks is extremely important. A homeowner buys a triplex for $650,000, puts 10% down, and has a mortgage of about $3,600 per month. After adding taxes, insurance, maintenance, and utilities, the total monthly cost of the property is about $5,200.

The homeowner rents out two units for $2,200 and $2,100 per month, earning $4,300 in rental income. This reduces their personal housing cost to only about $900 per month. On top of that, they decide to pay an extra $1,200 per month toward the mortgage, which helps them pay off the loan much faster than normal and build equity more quickly.

However, problems can happen in real life. In this example, one tenant moves out for three months, causing $6,300 in lost rent. On top of that, the homeowner also spends money on repairs and marketing, bringing the total financial setback to about $8,600. Without savings, this situation could create serious stress and force the homeowner to stop making extra mortgage payments or even rely on credit cards.

Because this homeowner planned ahead, they had emergency reserves. They were saving about 10% of rental income each month, which built up to over $10,000 in reserves after two years. This means they were able to cover all the vacancy and repair costs without stress, without debt, and without interrupting their mortgage payoff strategy.

Even after handling the setback, the homeowner still continues their accelerated plan. Over time, this allows them to pay off the mortgage in about 16 years instead of 30, saving around $345,000 in interest. At the same time, the property grows in value to about $1.22 million after 16 years, while the mortgage balance drops close to zero.

The key lesson is that real estate investing and house hacking only work well long-term when they are built with safety margins. Reserves, planning for vacancies, and budgeting for repairs are what allow the strategy to survive real-life problems. The goal is not to avoid challenges completely, but to build a financial system strong enough to keep growing even when problems happen.

Chapter 7

Building Long-Term Financial Freedom After the Mortgage Is Paid Off

For many homeowners, paying off the mortgage feels like the ultimate financial finish line. After years of making monthly payments, managing rental income, handling maintenance, and applying extra principal payments consistently, finally eliminating the mortgage can feel life-changing. The monthly burden that once dominated financial planning disappears. Cash flow improves dramatically. Stress levels decrease. Financial flexibility increases. However, one of the most important concepts successful homeowners eventually learn is that mortgage payoff is not the end of the journey—it is the beginning of an entirely new financial phase.

A paid-off property creates opportunities that many people never fully experience because they remain trapped in debt for most of their lives. Once the mortgage disappears, rental income that previously supported loan payments becomes available for wealth building, investments, business opportunities, retirement planning, travel, family support, or additional real estate acquisitions. The homeowner transitions from debt reduction mode into wealth expansion mode. At this stage, the financial system built through house hacking and rental income begins producing some of its most powerful long-term benefits.

One of the greatest advantages of owning property free and clear is dramatically improved monthly cash flow. Mortgage payments are usually the largest expense associated with real estate ownership. Once eliminated, the property still requires taxes, insurance, maintenance, and operational expenses, but the largest debt obligation disappears entirely. Rental income that once merely reduced housing costs now becomes a major source of positive monthly cash flow.

For example, a duplex generating $4,000 monthly rental income may have previously produced only modest positive cash flow while the mortgage existed. Once the mortgage is eliminated, however, the majority of that income may become available to the owner after operating expenses. This creates financial flexibility that can fundamentally transform the homeowner's lifestyle and long-term opportunities.

Cash flow freedom often changes how people think about work entirely. Many homeowners spend decades working primarily to support housing expenses. Once those obligations disappear, career decisions become more flexible. Some individuals reduce working hours, transition into passion-based careers, start businesses, travel more frequently, or retire earlier than they originally thought possible. Financial pressure decreases significantly because the monthly income required for survival becomes much lower.

One of the most important mindset shifts after mortgage payoff is understanding the difference between income and expenses. Many people focus entirely on increasing income throughout life while ignoring the importance of reducing fixed expenses. A homeowner with low living expenses often experiences greater financial stability than someone earning significantly more money but carrying heavy debt obligations. Eliminating the mortgage permanently reduces one of the largest recurring expenses most families will ever face.

Rental income from paid-off properties also creates opportunities for reinvestment. Some homeowners continue purchasing additional properties using cash flow generated from existing rentals. Others diversify into stock market investments, businesses, retirement accounts, or other income-producing assets. The key advantage is that paid-off real estate often creates recurring monthly cash flow capable of supporting multiple future wealth-building strategies simultaneously.

Another major advantage of mortgage freedom is increased resilience during economic uncertainty. Individuals carrying large monthly debt obligations often experience tremendous stress during recessions, job loss, health emergencies, or economic downturns. By contrast, homeowners with paid-off properties and rental income frequently maintain much stronger financial stability because their fixed obligations remain relatively low. This resilience creates emotional peace and long-term security.

Tax planning also becomes increasingly important after mortgage elimination. Many homeowners mistakenly assume eliminating debt automatically creates perfect financial outcomes in every situation. However, paid-off properties generate taxable income, and strategic planning becomes essential to maximize long-term efficiency. Depreciation schedules, maintenance expenses, property upgrades, business deductions, retirement contributions, and investment structures all influence long-term wealth preservation. Working with experienced tax professionals often becomes more valuable as cash flow and asset ownership increase.

Another powerful benefit of owning real estate free and clear is the ability to leverage opportunities selectively rather than out of necessity. A homeowner with strong equity and stable cash flow may choose to access equity strategically through lines of credit or refinancing for investments, business expansion, or property acquisitions. However, because the property itself is stable and profitable, the homeowner makes these decisions from positions of strength rather than financial desperation.

Many successful investors eventually focus heavily on lifestyle design once mortgage freedom is achieved. During earlier stages of wealth building, aggressive saving, house hacking, tenant management, and debt reduction may require discipline and temporary sacrifices. But eventually, the financial system begins supporting greater personal freedom. Time becomes more valuable than money alone. Family experiences, health, travel, hobbies, and flexibility often become higher priorities because financial pressure has decreased substantially.

The emotional transformation after mortgage payoff can be profound. Many homeowners spend years carrying constant financial anxiety related to housing expenses. Even individuals earning strong incomes may quietly fear job loss or economic instability because large monthly mortgage payments create ongoing pressure. Eliminating the mortgage often creates psychological relief that extends far beyond simple mathematics.

Parents frequently experience additional peace of mind

knowing their family home is secure regardless of future income fluctuations. Retirement planning also becomes dramatically easier when housing costs are minimal. Individuals no longer need to generate the same level of monthly income to maintain stability, which often allows retirement savings to last much longer.

Some homeowners choose to continue operating house hacking strategies even after achieving mortgage freedom. For example, someone living in one unit of a paid-off duplex may continue collecting rent from the other unit indefinitely, effectively living at extremely low cost while generating ongoing income. Others transition fully into investment property ownership by moving into new homes while retaining former properties as rentals.

One important lesson many financially successful homeowners eventually learn is that real estate wealth compounds over long periods of time. Appreciation, rising rents, debt reduction, tax advantages, and cash flow often accelerate significantly after years of ownership. Many people underestimate how dramatically wealth can grow once mortgage obligations disappear and rental income continues increasing.

Inflation also works differently for paid-off property owners. Rising housing costs often hurt renters and heavily leveraged homeowners. However, owners of fixed-rate or paid-off properties frequently benefit because rents and property values may continue increasing while debt obligations remain stable or nonexistent. This creates expanding cash flow margins over time. Another major opportunity after mortgage payoff involves legacy planning and generational wealth creation. Paid-off real estate can provide long-term stability not only for the current owner but also for future generations. Rental income may support children's education, family businesses, retirement security, or inheritance planning. Properties held over long periods often become significant family assets capable of creating opportunities far beyond the original purchase price.

However, maintaining discipline remains important even after mortgage elimination. Some homeowners experience "financial drift" once major debt disappears and begin increasing spending excessively. Luxury purchases, lifestyle inflation, unnecessary debt, or poor investments can quickly reduce the advantages created through years of disciplined financial management. Sustainable wealth requires continued intentionality even after achieving major milestones.

Property management standards should also remain high after mortgage payoff. Some owners become complacent once properties are free and clear, neglecting maintenance, tenant quality, or operational efficiency. However, protecting property value and rental demand remains essential for preserving long-term cash flow and appreciation potential.

Insurance, legal protection, estate planning, and liability management also become increasingly important as wealth grows. Many successful property owners establish LLCs, umbrella insurance policies, trusts, or estate plans to protect assets and simplify long-term wealth transfer strategies. Professional guidance often becomes more important as asset values increase.

One of the most overlooked aspects of financial freedom is optionality. Homeowners with strong cash flow and low debt gain the ability to make decisions based on opportunity rather than necessity. They can relocate, pursue entrepreneurship, reduce working hours, help family members, travel, volunteer, or explore new goals without the same financial constraints affecting heavily indebted households.

The concept of "time freedom" often becomes more valuable than income alone. Many individuals spend decades sacrificing time, health, and relationships to support large debt obligations. Mortgage freedom allows homeowners to reclaim increasing amounts of control over their schedules and priorities. This shift often creates greater life satisfaction than material purchases alone.

Another advantage of paid-off rental properties is flexibility during market fluctuations. Investors carrying heavy leverage may feel forced to sell during downturns due to cash flow pressure or financing challenges. By contrast, owners of stable paid-off properties can often hold long term comfortably while continuing collecting income and waiting for market recovery.

Ultimately, the purpose of house hacking and rental income strategies extends far beyond simply paying off a mortgage early. The larger goal is creating a financial structure capable of supporting long-term freedom, security, flexibility, and opportunity. Mortgage payoff is simply one milestone within a broader wealth-building journey.

The homeowner who successfully eliminates debt using rental income gains far more than a paid-off property. They gain knowledge, discipline, systems, confidence, and financial flexibility that can continue creating opportunities for decades. What began as a strategy to reduce housing expenses often evolves into a completely different relationship with money, work, and life itself.

The most important realization is this: financial freedom is rarely created through one giant moment. It is usually built gradually through consistent decisions repeated over many years. One extra payment. One rental property. One disciplined system. One strategic purchase. Over time, those decisions compound into extraordinary results.

A paid-off property is not merely a piece of real estate. It represents years of intentional financial behavior transformed into stability, opportunity, and freedom. For many homeowners, that freedom becomes one of the most valuable assets they will ever possess.

Life After Paying Off the Mortgage with Rental Income

This example shows how a homeowner can use house hacking to eventually reach financial freedom. They buy a fourplex for $800,000 with a 10% down payment, leaving a $720,000 mortgage at 6% interest. The monthly mortgage payment is about $4,317, and after adding taxes, insurance, and maintenance, total expenses are about $6,067 per month.

The homeowner rents out three units for a total of about $6,100 per month. This means the rental income almost completely covers the property expenses, allowing the homeowner to live in one unit at very low cost. On top of that, they decide to add an extra $2,000 per month toward the mortgage, helping them pay it off much faster.

Because of this strategy, the mortgage is paid off in about 14 years instead of 30. This saves nearly $484,000 in interest over time. Instead of paying over $800,000 in interest, the homeowner only pays about $350,000, which is a huge financial difference created by extra payments and rental income. Over those 14 years, the property also increases in value. With 4% annual appreciation, the $800,000 property grows to about $1.38 million. At the same time, the mortgage balance drops to zero, meaning the homeowner now owns the entire property free and clear.

Rental income also grows over time. By year 14, rents increase to about $9,100 per month. Even after paying higher expenses like taxes, insurance, and maintenance (about $2,450 per month), the property still generates around $6,650 per month in positive cash flow, or nearly $80,000 per year.

The key lesson is that house hacking does more than reduce housing costs—it can completely transform a property into a long-term wealth-building machine. By combining rental income, aggressive mortgage payoff, appreciation, and disciplined planning, a homeowner can turn one property into a debt-free asset that produces strong cash flow and supports long-term financial freedom.

Chapter 8

Advanced Strategies to Maximize Rental Income and Accelerate Mortgage Freedom

Once homeowners understand the foundations of house hacking, rental cash flow management, mortgage acceleration, and long-term wealth building, they often begin searching for ways to optimize results even further. At this stage, the focus shifts from simply reducing housing expenses toward maximizing efficiency, increasing profitability, and creating stronger long-term financial leverage. Advanced strategies allow homeowners to accelerate mortgage payoff timelines dramatically while building additional streams of income and increasing overall property performance.

Many homeowners stop after implementing basic rental strategies. They collect rent, cover expenses, and slowly reduce their mortgage over time. While this approach alone can create tremendous financial improvement, advanced investors understand that small operational adjustments often create substantial increases in cash flow, equity growth, and long-term wealth accumulation. The difference between average and exceptional real estate performance frequently comes down to optimization.

One of the most powerful advanced strategies involves increasing income without dramatically increasing expenses. Many homeowners focus only on reducing costs, but expanding revenue opportunities often creates far greater financial impact. A property generating additional rental income while maintaining relatively stable expenses can accelerate mortgage payoff much faster than simple cost-cutting alone.

Room-by-room rentals represent one method many investors use to increase cash flow significantly. In some markets, renting individual rooms separately generates substantially more income than leasing an entire property to a single tenant. College towns, healthcare markets, military communities, and urban employment centers often create strong demand for affordable shared housing arrangements. A homeowner who strategically structures room rentals may generate thousands of dollars in additional annual income compared to traditional lease models.

Accessory dwelling units, commonly called ADUs, have also become increasingly popular. These are secondary living spaces added to existing properties, such as garage apartments, detached guest houses, converted basements, or backyard cottages. In many markets, ADUs create powerful additional income streams while increasing property value simultaneously. Some homeowners are able to generate enough income from an ADU alone to cover substantial portions of their mortgage payment.

Short-term rental optimization provides another advanced strategy for maximizing income potential. Many homeowners initially enter short-term rentals casually without fully understanding pricing optimization, occupancy management, guest experience systems, or seasonal demand trends. Professional operators often dramatically outperform average hosts by strategically managing listings, reviews, amenities, photography, marketing, and dynamic pricing.

For example, improving listing photos, upgrading internet speed, adding premium furnishings, automating guest communication, or creating unique guest experiences can significantly increase occupancy rates and nightly pricing. Small improvements in average occupancy and pricing often create surprisingly large increases in annual revenue.

Another advanced strategy involves combining multiple rental models within the same property. A homeowner may use long-term rentals for stability in certain units while operating short-term rentals in others for higher cash flow potential.

Some investors rent rooms to traveling nurses, business professionals, or students on medium-term contracts that balance income potential with reduced turnover frequency. Hybrid approaches often provide both flexibility and diversification.

Mortgage optimization itself also becomes increasingly important as investors grow more experienced. Refinancing into lower interest rates, shorter loan terms, or improved financing structures can significantly accelerate long-term wealth creation. However, refinancing decisions should always consider total long-term costs rather than focusing solely on monthly payment reductions.

For example, shortening a mortgage term from thirty years to fifteen years may increase monthly payments temporarily but dramatically reduce total interest expenses and accelerate equity growth. Homeowners with strong rental income and improving cash flow may strategically choose shorter loan structures once properties become more stable financially.

Biweekly payment strategies can also create additional mortgage acceleration. Instead of making one monthly payment, homeowners make half-payments every two weeks. Because there are twenty-six biweekly periods annually, this effectively creates one additional full mortgage payment per year. Over time, this relatively simple adjustment can reduce loan timelines substantially.

Another advanced concept involves "equity recycling." As homeowners build equity through appreciation and principal reduction, they may strategically access portions of that equity to acquire additional income-producing assets. However, this strategy requires careful discipline and conservative financial analysis. Excessive leverage creates risk, but strategic leverage can accelerate portfolio growth when managed responsibly.

Tax strategy optimization also becomes more valuable at advanced stages of real estate ownership. Many homeowners initially overlook deductions related to depreciation, maintenance, repairs, utilities, insurance, business mileage, home office usage, management expenses, and property operations. Working with knowledgeable tax professionals often reveals opportunities to improve after-tax cash flow significantly.

Depreciation represents one of the most powerful tax benefits available to real estate investors. Even though properties may appreciate in actual market value, portions of the property can often be depreciated for tax purposes over time. This accounting benefit may reduce taxable income substantially while the property itself continues increasing in value and generating cash flow. Another advanced strategy involves improving tenant quality and retention systems. Many landlords focus heavily on increasing rent while ignoring the financial value of stable, reliable tenants. Frequent turnover creates vacancy costs, repairs, marketing expenses, and operational stress. Investors who build strong tenant relationships, maintain properties well, communicate professionally, and create positive living environments often achieve stronger long-term profitability through lower turnover rates.

Property upgrades can also increase rental income strategically. Not every renovation creates strong financial returns, but targeted improvements often generate substantial value. Updated kitchens, modern flooring, improved landscaping, in-unit laundry, energy-efficient appliances, smart home features, parking improvements, and upgraded bathrooms may justify higher rents while improving tenant satisfaction.

However, successful investors carefully analyze return on investment before completing upgrades. Spending $50,000 on renovations that only increase rent slightly may create weak returns. The goal is maximizing profitability rather than simply creating luxury properties unnecessarily.

Market analysis becomes increasingly important as homeowners expand advanced strategies. Understanding local supply and demand trends, population growth, zoning changes, employment expansion, infrastructure projects, and neighborhood development helps investors identify opportunities earlier than the general public. Real estate markets often reward investors who recognize emerging trends before prices fully adjust.

Time management also becomes critical at advanced stages. Many homeowners initially manage everything themselves to maximize cash flow. However, as portfolios grow or personal priorities change, outsourcing certain tasks may improve overall lifestyle quality and operational efficiency. Cleaning services, property managers, bookkeepers, contractors, virtual assistants, and automation systems may reduce stress while preserving scalability.

Asset protection strategies also become more important as wealth grows. Limited liability companies, umbrella insurance policies, estate planning structures, trusts, and legal protections help reduce long-term risk exposure. Protecting accumulated wealth becomes just as important as creating it initially.

One advanced mindset shift many successful investors eventually adopt is focusing on "financial velocity." Instead of simply earning money and slowly saving it, they focus on directing cash flow strategically toward appreciating or income-producing assets repeatedly. Rental income accelerates mortgage reduction. Reduced mortgage obligations increase available cash flow. Additional cash flow supports investments. Investments create more income. This cycle compounds over time into substantial wealth.

The concept of opportunity cost also becomes increasingly relevant. Every financial decision carries trade-offs. Extra cash flow may be directed toward mortgage payoff, investments, business growth, property upgrades, retirement accounts, or reserve expansion. Advanced investors evaluate where each dollar creates the strongest long-term financial impact while balancing risk and stability.

Inflation management represents another advanced advantage of real estate ownership. Homeowners with fixed-rate debt and growing rental income often benefit significantly during inflationary periods. As rents rise over time, cash flow increases while fixed mortgage payments remain stable. This creates expanding profit margins that can accelerate financial freedom dramatically.

Many advanced investors eventually transition from thinking only about monthly cash flow toward evaluating total wealth creation. Appreciation, tax savings, principal reduction, cash flow growth, refinancing opportunities, and portfolio scalability all combine into long-term net worth expansion. Real estate wealth often compounds slowly at first and then accelerates dramatically over longer ownership periods.

However, discipline remains essential throughout every advanced strategy. Some investors become overconfident during strong markets and abandon conservative financial principles. Excessive leverage, poor reserve management, speculative purchases, or uncontrolled expansion can quickly destroy years of financial progress. Sustainable success depends on balancing ambition with stability consistently.

One of the greatest advantages of advanced rental income strategies is optionality. Homeowners who optimize cash flow and reduce mortgage obligations gain increasing control over their future. They can pursue entrepreneurship, travel, career changes, early retirement, or family priorities with far greater flexibility than heavily indebted households dependent solely on employment income.

Ultimately, advanced real estate strategies are not only about maximizing money. They are about maximizing freedom, flexibility, and long-term control over life decisions. A property generating optimized cash flow while reducing debt rapidly creates opportunities far beyond simple homeownership alone.

The homeowner who masters advanced rental income strategies eventually stops viewing real estate merely as housing. Instead, they see property as a financial system capable of generating cash flow, reducing debt, building equity, protecting against inflation, supporting investments, and creating lasting long-term wealth. That transformation in thinking often becomes the foundation for extraordinary financial freedom.

Advanced Rental Optimization to Accelerate Mortgage Freedom

This example shows how improving and optimizing a rental property can dramatically increase income and speed up mortgage payoff. A homeowner buys a $700,000 home with a $630,000 mortgage at 6.25% interest. The monthly mortgage payment is about $3,880, and after taxes, insurance, and utilities, total monthly costs are about $5,500.

At first, the homeowner uses a simple house hacking strategy by renting out two spare bedrooms for $1,000 each. This brings in $2,000 per month in rental income, lowering their real housing cost to about $3,500 per month. This already makes the property much more affordable compared to paying everything alone.

After one year, the homeowner upgrades the property to increase income. They convert the garage into a studio apartment that rents for $1,800 per month. They also improve one bedroom rental by turning it into a furnished medium-term rental, increasing its rent from $1,000 to $1,400 per month. These upgrades significantly boost total rental income.

After optimization, total rental income increases to about $4,200 per month. This reduces the homeowner's real housing cost to only about $1,300 per month. Because expenses are now so low, the homeowner is able to put an extra $2,500 per month directly toward paying down the mortgage.

With this strategy, the mortgage is paid off in about 11 years and 9 months instead of 30 years. This saves approximately $520,000 in interest compared to a traditional payoff schedule. At the same time, the property grows in value to about $1.12 million after 12 years, while the mortgage balance drops close to zero.

After the mortgage is paid off, rental income continues to grow and becomes strong monthly cash flow. Even after expenses, the property generates about $3,300 per month, or roughly $39,600 per year in passive income. The key lesson is that small improvements—like adding rental units, increasing rent efficiency, and reinvesting cash flow—can transform a single home into a powerful long-term wealth-building asset that leads to financial freedom.

Chapter 9

Balancing Mortgage Payoff with Building a Real Estate Portfolio

One of the biggest financial decisions homeowners eventually face after successfully using rental income and house hacking strategies is determining how to balance aggressive mortgage payoff with expanding into additional real estate investments. At first, the answer may seem obvious. Many people naturally assume eliminating debt as quickly as possible should always be the highest priority. Others believe maximizing leverage and acquiring as many properties as possible creates the fastest path to wealth. In reality, both approaches contain advantages, risks, and trade-offs. The most successful long-term investors usually learn how to balance debt reduction with strategic portfolio growth in ways that align with their financial goals, personality, risk tolerance, and lifestyle priorities.

The idea of paying off a mortgage early creates emotional security for many homeowners. Eliminating debt reduces monthly obligations, lowers financial stress, and increases stability during uncertain economic conditions. A paid-off property can provide tremendous peace of mind because housing costs decrease dramatically. For many families, mortgage freedom represents safety and long-term security more than simply mathematics.

At the same time, real estate itself often creates wealth through leverage. Mortgage financing allows investors to control valuable assets using relatively small amounts of initial capital. Appreciation occurs based on the full property value rather than only the original down payment. Rental income supports debt reduction while tenants indirectly help build equity over time. Because of this leverage effect, some investors choose to maintain low-interest mortgage debt while using available capital to acquire additional income-producing properties.

The challenge is that there is no universal answer suitable for every homeowner. The ideal strategy depends on multiple factors including age, income stability, investment experience, interest rates, cash flow strength, market conditions, retirement goals, and emotional comfort with debt. Some people sleep better knowing their properties are paid off quickly. Others are comfortable using moderate leverage to accelerate portfolio growth. Understanding both perspectives is critical for making intelligent long-term financial decisions.

One of the most important concepts in balancing mortgage payoff with portfolio expansion is opportunity cost. Every extra dollar applied toward mortgage principal is a dollar that cannot simultaneously be used for another investment opportunity. If a homeowner aggressively pays down a low-interest mortgage but misses the opportunity to purchase a strong cash-flowing property, the long-term financial outcome may differ significantly compared to someone who prioritized expansion.

For example, imagine a homeowner with strong rental income generating substantial monthly cash flow. They may choose between aggressively paying down a 5% mortgage or using available capital as a down payment for another income-producing property generating higher overall returns. In some situations, acquiring additional assets may produce greater long-term wealth than eliminating low-cost debt rapidly. However, additional properties also increase complexity, leverage exposure, and operational responsibilities.

Cash flow becomes the foundation of every intelligent decision in this process. Positive cash flow creates flexibility regardless of strategy. A homeowner with stable rental income and manageable debt obligations usually maintains far greater financial resilience than someone with highly leveraged properties producing weak or negative cash flow. Sustainable investing always prioritizes stability over speculation.

One major advantage of balancing debt reduction with portfolio growth is diversification of income streams. A homeowner with multiple properties generating cash flow from different tenants or markets may reduce reliance on any single income source. If one property experiences vacancy temporarily, other properties may continue supporting overall financial stability. Multiple income streams often create stronger long-term resilience than relying entirely on one paid-off property alone.

At the same time, carrying too much debt across multiple properties can create substantial risk during economic downturns, rising interest rates, or prolonged vacancies. Some investors become overly aggressive during strong markets, assuming rents and property values will continue rising indefinitely. When market conditions shift, excessive leverage can quickly create financial pressure. The 2008 housing crisis demonstrated how dangerous overleveraging can become when investors ignore cash flow fundamentals and reserve management.

This is why conservative leverage and strong reserves remain essential regardless of portfolio size. Successful investors typically avoid stretching themselves to maximum loan approval amounts. Instead, they maintain safety margins allowing properties to remain stable even during temporary disruptions.

Another important factor involves interest rates. Low fixed-rate mortgage debt often becomes more attractive to maintain when inflation rises and rents continue increasing. In these situations, the real cost of debt may effectively decline over time while property cash flow improves. Some investors intentionally maintain long-term low-interest mortgages while investing available cash elsewhere because inflation gradually reduces the real burden of fixed payments.

However, higher interest rates change the equation significantly. Expensive debt reduces cash flow and increases financial risk. In high-rate environments, aggressively reducing debt may produce stronger guaranteed returns compared to uncertain investment opportunities elsewhere. Mortgage strategy should always consider the financing environment carefully.

Age and life stage also influence decision-making. Younger investors with stable careers and long investment timelines may tolerate more leverage and portfolio expansion because they have decades to recover from market fluctuations and benefit from appreciation. Meanwhile, individuals approaching retirement often prioritize debt reduction, stability, and predictable cash flow. Eliminating mortgage obligations before retirement frequently reduces financial pressure and lowers required retirement income substantially. Lifestyle goals matter just as much as financial calculations. Some investors enjoy building and managing growing portfolios. Others prefer simplicity and peace of mind. A large portfolio with substantial leverage may produce impressive theoretical returns but also create stress, management demands, and operational complexity. By contrast, smaller portfolios with lower debt may create greater lifestyle freedom despite slower expansion.

Many successful homeowners eventually adopt hybrid strategies balancing both objectives simultaneously. Instead of directing every dollar exclusively toward either mortgage payoff or new acquisitions, they allocate portions toward each goal strategically. For example, they may aggressively reduce debt on one property while saving for another purchase gradually. Others acquire properties during strong opportunities while later focusing on accelerated debt reduction once cash flow improves.

Refinancing strategies also influence portfolio growth decisions. As properties appreciate and mortgage balances decline, homeowners may access equity through cash-out refinancing or home equity lines of credit. These funds may support additional property purchases, renovations, or investments. However, accessing equity increases leverage again, which reintroduces risk. Responsible investors evaluate cash flow carefully before recycling equity into new acquisitions. Tax considerations also affect the mortgage-versus-expansion decision. Mortgage interest may provide deductions under certain circumstances, while rental properties create depreciation opportunities and business-related write-offs. Investors often work with accountants or tax advisors to structure acquisitions and debt management efficiently based on their specific financial situations.

Another important concept is velocity of wealth creation. Paying off one mortgage completely creates tremendous stability, but multiple appreciating cash-flowing properties may potentially accelerate net worth growth faster over long periods. Appreciation compounds across all owned assets simultaneously. Meanwhile, tenants continue contributing toward mortgage reduction across multiple properties. Over decades, even moderate appreciation on several leveraged properties can create substantial wealth expansion.

However, appreciation alone should never become the primary justification for aggressive investing. Markets fluctuate, and appreciation is never guaranteed short term. Investors who rely entirely on appreciation while ignoring cash flow often experience major problems during market corrections. Sustainable portfolios are built on strong cash flow first, with appreciation treated as an additional long-term advantage rather than the sole strategy. Emotional discipline becomes extremely important during expansion phases. Some investors become addicted to acquiring properties and lose focus on stability, reserves, or long-term sustainability. Others become overly fearful of debt and miss opportunities to create meaningful wealth through strategic investments. Long-term success usually comes from balanced thinking rather than emotional extremes.

Time management also changes significantly as portfolios grow. Managing one duplex differs greatly from managing multiple multifamily properties, short-term rentals, or geographically dispersed investments. Some homeowners eventually hire property managers to reduce operational responsibilities. Others intentionally maintain smaller portfolios to preserve lifestyle flexibility and reduce stress.

One overlooked benefit of balancing debt reduction with investing is optionality. Investors maintaining strong equity, healthy cash flow, and manageable leverage gain increasing flexibility over time. They can accelerate payoff if markets weaken, expand aggressively during opportunities, or shift strategies depending on changing goals and economic conditions. Financial flexibility often becomes more valuable than maximizing theoretical returns alone.

Long-term wealth building through real estate rarely follows a perfectly linear path. Some years focus heavily on acquisition. Other years prioritize stabilization, debt reduction, reserve building, or renovations. Successful investors adapt continuously rather than blindly following rigid formulas.

One critical realization many investors eventually reach is that financial freedom depends less on the number of properties owned and more on the relationship between income, debt, expenses, and time flexibility. Someone owning ten heavily leveraged stressful properties may feel less financially free than someone owning three stable low-debt cash-flowing properties generating reliable income.

House hacking provides an exceptional starting point because it allows homeowners to enter real estate investing gradually while reducing personal housing costs dramatically. Over time, homeowners can decide whether they prefer aggressive expansion, debt elimination, or balanced hybrid strategies. The experience gained from the first property often shapes future investment philosophy significantly.

Ultimately, the goal is not simply owning real estate or eliminating mortgages quickly in isolation. The goal is building a financial structure supporting long-term security, flexibility, and freedom. Whether that structure emphasizes faster debt payoff, broader portfolio growth, or balanced progression depends entirely on the homeowner's unique priorities and vision for life. The most successful long-term investors understand that wealth building is not a race against others. It is a process of creating sustainable systems aligned with personal values, risk tolerance, and long-term goals. Real estate becomes most powerful when it supports not only financial growth but also peace of mind, flexibility, and quality of life.

Paying Off One Property vs. Building a Portfolio

This example compares two homeowners who both buy the same duplex for $500,000 using a 10% down payment and a $450,000 mortgage at 6% interest. Their monthly mortgage payment is about $2,698, and after adding taxes, insurance, and maintenance, total expenses are about $3,698 per month. They rent out the second unit for $2,200, which reduces their real housing cost to about $1,498 per month.

Investor A chooses an aggressive strategy focused on paying off the mortgage as fast as possible. They add an extra $2,000 per month toward the loan, bringing their total payment to about $4,698 per month. This allows them to pay off the mortgage in about 11 years and 10 months, saving roughly $334,000 in interest over time.

By the end of the period, Investor A owns the property free and clear. With 4% annual appreciation, the duplex grows to about $800,000 in value after 12 years. This gives them strong financial security, low housing costs, and a simple financial situation, but they do not build additional properties or income streams during this time.

Investor B takes a different approach. Instead of putting most extra money toward the mortgage, they only add $500 per month and use the rest to save for future investments. Because of this, their mortgage takes longer to pay off, about 22 years, but they are able to grow a larger real estate portfolio.

After four years, Investor B buys a second property, a triplex for $700,000 with a 20% down payment. This property generates about $6,000 per month in rent and produces around $1,300 in positive monthly cash flow after expenses. Over time, both properties grow in value, with the duplex reaching about $800,000 and the triplex about $960,000 after 12 years.

In the end, Investor A has a fully paid-off home worth about $800,000, while Investor B has a larger portfolio worth about

$1.76 million with multiple income streams and about $1.04 million in equity. The key lesson is that both strategies can work—one focuses on simplicity and debt freedom, while the other focuses on growth and cash flow. The best choice depends on personal goals, risk tolerance, and whether someone values stability or expansion more.

Chapter 10

The Ultimate Mortgage Payoff Game Plan – Combining All Strategies Into Financial Freedom

At this stage of the Mortgage Payoff & Wealth Acceleration Series, the homeowner has already learned the foundational principles of house hacking, rental income optimization, mortgage acceleration, risk management, scaling strategies, advanced income techniques, and portfolio balancing. The final step is learning how to bring all of these strategies together into one cohesive, long-term game plan that creates predictable progress toward financial freedom. The ultimate mortgage payoff system is not a single tactic or shortcut. It is the combination of disciplined cash flow management, strategic real estate use, and long-term financial planning applied consistently over time.

Most homeowners begin their journey by focusing only on one strategy at a time. They may start by simply trying to pay extra on their mortgage. Others begin by renting a portion of their home without any structured plan. Some may purchase a small multifamily property but fail to integrate the income into a broader financial system. While each of these actions can produce benefits individually, the most powerful results occur when all strategies are combined into a unified system.

The ultimate game plan begins with understanding your current financial position. Every homeowner must first evaluate income, expenses, debt obligations, property equity, interest rates, and available savings. Without a clear baseline, it becomes impossible to measure progress or design an effective strategy. Financial awareness is the foundation of all long-term wealth creation.

Once the financial baseline is understood, the next step is identifying immediate opportunities for house hacking or rental income. This may involve renting unused rooms, converting basement spaces, adding accessory dwelling units, or purchasing a multifamily property. The goal is to create immediate cash flow that reduces housing expenses and increases financial flexibility.

Cash flow is the engine that powers the entire system. Without positive cash flow, mortgage acceleration becomes significantly more difficult because homeowners must rely solely on employment income. With rental income, however, the financial system becomes multi-dimensional. Income is no longer limited to a single source. Instead, multiple streams work together to reduce debt, build equity, and create long-term wealth.

The next layer of the game plan involves disciplined allocation of cash flow. Instead of spending rental income without structure, successful homeowners divide income into specific categories. A portion goes toward mortgage principal reduction. A portion goes into emergency reserves. A portion may be allocated to maintenance or repairs. Another portion may be saved for future investment opportunities. This structured approach ensures that rental income is always working toward long-term goals rather than short-term consumption.

Consistency is one of the most powerful elements of the ultimate mortgage payoff system. Small, repeated actions over long periods of time create extraordinary financial results. An extra $500 or $1,000 applied consistently toward mortgage principal each month may seem modest at first, but over time it can reduce loan timelines by many years and save hundreds of thousands of dollars in interest.

Automation plays a critical role in maintaining consistency. When systems are automated, financial discipline no longer depends on daily decision-making. Rent is collected automatically. Transfers to savings occur automatically. Extra mortgage payments are scheduled automatically. This removes emotional interference and ensures that the strategy continues operating even when life becomes busy or unpredictable.

Another essential component of the ultimate game plan is leveraging equity strategically. As homeowners build equity through appreciation and principal reduction, they gain access to financial tools such as refinancing or home equity lines of credit. These tools can be used to acquire additional income-producing properties or strengthen cash reserves. However, this step must be handled carefully to avoid overleveraging. Equity is a powerful tool, but it must be used with discipline.

At the same time, homeowners must continuously evaluate their risk exposure. Vacancy rates, tenant stability, maintenance costs, insurance coverage, and market conditions all affect long-term performance. The ultimate strategy always includes strong reserves and conservative planning to ensure stability during economic fluctuations. A financially secure system is one that continues functioning even when unexpected challenges arise.

One of the most powerful aspects of combining all strategies is compounding. Mortgage reduction creates equity. Equity creates borrowing power. Borrowing power creates additional investments. Additional investments create more cash flow.

More cash flow accelerates mortgage payoff even further. This cycle compounds over time and becomes increasingly powerful as the system matures.

Tax efficiency also plays a significant role in the ultimate game plan. Real estate offers numerous tax advantages including depreciation, expense deductions, interest write-offs, and business-related reductions. When combined with rental income and mortgage acceleration, these tax benefits significantly improve after-tax cash flow and long-term wealth accumulation.

Another important factor is lifestyle alignment. Financial strategies must support the homeowner's desired lifestyle rather than restrict it. The ultimate mortgage payoff plan should not create burnout, stress, or emotional exhaustion. Instead, it should create freedom, flexibility, and long-term stability. A sustainable system is far more powerful than an aggressive system that cannot be maintained.

Time horizon also matters significantly. The ultimate game plan is not designed for overnight results. It is designed for long-term transformation over five, ten, fifteen, or even thirty years. Many homeowners underestimate the power of long-term consistency. Real estate wealth is built gradually through appreciation, leverage, cash flow, and disciplined financial behavior repeated over decades. As the system matures, homeowners often experience a shift in mindset. Initially, the mortgage feels like a burden that must be eliminated. Over time, it becomes a tool that is strategically managed. Eventually, the focus expands beyond the mortgage entirely toward total financial independence, portfolio growth, and legacy creation.

One of the final stages of the ultimate game plan is optionality. Financial optionality means having the ability to choose without financial pressure. A homeowner with strong equity, low debt, and consistent rental income can choose to work less, invest more aggressively, relocate, start a business, or retire early. This flexibility becomes one of the most valuable outcomes of the entire system.

Legacy planning also becomes increasingly important. Properties that are fully paid off or highly profitable can be passed to future generations, creating long-term financial stability for families. Real estate becomes not just a personal wealth tool, but a generational asset capable of producing income for decades.

Ultimately, the mortgage payoff journey is not about one strategy or one decision. It is about building a system that integrates multiple financial principles into a cohesive plan.

House hacking creates entry. Rental income creates cash flow. Discipline creates consistency. Risk management creates stability. Scaling creates growth. Advanced strategies create optimization. And long-term planning creates freedom.

The ultimate mortgage payoff game plan works because it transforms real estate from a simple asset into a complete financial system. Instead of relying solely on employment income or short-term savings, homeowners create an interconnected structure where each component strengthens the others over time.

The result is not just a paid-off mortgage. The result is a financial ecosystem capable of generating income, building wealth, reducing risk, and supporting long-term freedom. When executed correctly, this system can fundamentally change the trajectory of a family's financial future for generations.

The Complete Mortgage Payoff System in Action

This example combines all the strategies from the series into one real long-term plan. A homeowner buys a $550,000 home using a 10% down payment and a $495,000 mortgage at 6.25% interest. The monthly mortgage payment is about $3,050, and with taxes and insurance, total housing costs are about $3,950 per month.

The homeowner uses house hacking to reduce their living expenses. They rent out a basement apartment for $1,800 and a spare bedroom for $1,000, earning $2,800 per month in rental income. This reduces their real housing cost to only about $1,150 per month, making the property very affordable to hold.

With this extra savings, the homeowner adds $1,500 per month toward the mortgage principal. This increases their total payment to about $4,550 per month and significantly speeds up the payoff timeline. Instead of taking 30 years, the mortgage is paid off in about 14 years.

After three years, the homeowner uses equity and savings to buy a second property—a duplex for $650,000. This property generates about $4,900 per month in rent and produces around $900 per month in positive cash flow after expenses. Now the homeowner has both reduced living costs and a growing investment portfolio.

Over the long term, both properties grow in value. After about 14 years, the first home is worth around $1.1 million and the second property about $1.3 million, creating a total real estate portfolio of roughly $2.4 million. Combined rental income reaches about $9,700 per month, and after expenses, the homeowner earns around $7,700 per month in net cash flow.

The key lesson is that real wealth does not come from just one strategy. It comes from combining house hacking, rental income, smart debt reduction, and strategic investing over time. When these systems work together, a mortgage is no longer just a debt—it becomes a tool that helps build long-term financial independence and generational wealth.

Final Tips and Suggestions for Mortgage Freedom

Reaching mortgage freedom is not just a financial milestone—it is a structural shift in how your entire life operates. For most homeowners, the mortgage represents decades of predictable pressure, a fixed monthly obligation that quietly shapes every career decision, spending habit, and long-term plan. Eliminating it does more than remove a payment; it changes your relationship with money, time, and opportunity. The final stage of this journey is about refinement, sustainability, and making sure the freedom you build is protected, scalable, and long-lasting rather than temporary or fragile.

One of the most important final lessons is that mortgage freedom is not created by one dramatic decision but by hundreds of small, disciplined actions repeated over time. Extra principal payments, consistent rental income management, careful tenant selection, conservative leverage, and strategic reinvestment all work together. The homeowners who succeed long term are rarely the ones who chase the fastest results. They are the ones who stay consistent when progress feels slow. Real estate rewards patience more than intensity.

A critical final principle is understanding that freedom does not mean stopping your system once the mortgage is paid off. Many homeowners make the mistake of celebrating financial freedom and then allowing lifestyle inflation to absorb all new cash flow. When that happens, the system collapses back into dependency. True mortgage freedom is not just eliminating debt—it is building a structure that continues generating surplus cash flow afterward. The goal is not just to escape the mortgage. The goal is to replace it with income-producing assets that continue growing your net worth.

Another essential tip is to protect your financial reserves at all times, even after achieving major milestones. Mortgage-free properties still require maintenance, insurance, taxes, and occasional repairs. Many investors become overconfident after eliminating debt and reduce their liquidity too aggressively. This creates unnecessary vulnerability. A strong reserve system is what allows freedom to remain freedom during unexpected events like job loss, market downturns, or property repairs. Cash reserves are not idle money—they are stability insurance.

It is also important to continue thinking in terms of systems rather than emotions. Emotional decision-making is one of the biggest threats to long-term financial success. After achieving mortgage freedom, homeowners often feel tempted to dramatically increase spending because pressure has been removed. However, disciplined investors understand that every dollar still has a job. Even without a mortgage, that money can be directed toward investments, retirement accounts, new properties, or income-generating opportunities. The system should evolve, not disappear.

Another powerful long-term principle is leveraging inflation instead of fearing it. Over time, inflation tends to increase rents, property values, and replacement costs. Homeowners with paid-off or heavily reduced mortgages are often in a position where their fixed housing costs are minimal while rental income continues rising. This creates expanding profit margins over time. Instead of being harmed by inflation like many consumers, real estate owners often benefit from it when structured correctly.

One of the most overlooked aspects of mortgage freedom is lifestyle alignment. Financial success without lifestyle alignment often leads to burnout or dissatisfaction. The purpose of building wealth is not simply to accumulate assets, but to improve quality of life. Once mortgage pressure is removed, homeowners should intentionally redesign their lives around their priorities. That may include more travel, more family time, reduced work hours, or pursuing meaningful projects that were previously impossible due to financial stress.

A strong suggestion for long-term success is to avoid overcomplicating your system. Many homeowners fall into the trap of constantly switching strategies, chasing new trends, or reacting emotionally to market noise. Simplicity often produces better results than complexity. A few well-executed strategies—consistent rental income, disciplined savings, conservative leverage, and steady investing—usually outperform complicated systems that are difficult to maintain over time.

Another key principle is to continue expanding financial literacy even after achieving mortgage freedom. Real estate markets evolve. Financing options change. Tax laws shift. Investment opportunities develop. The homeowners who continue learning remain adaptable and resilient. Those who stop learning often become stagnant or overly dependent on outdated strategies. Education is what keeps financial freedom sustainable across decades, not just years.

At this stage, it is also important to think about legacy. Mortgage freedom is not just about your current life—it is about what you leave behind. Paid-off properties, rental portfolios, and income-producing assets can become powerful generational tools. Many families build long-term wealth not through high income alone, but through strategic asset ownership passed down over time. Estate planning, wills, trusts, and tax-efficient structures become increasingly important as wealth grows. Another important final tip is to maintain humility during success. One of the biggest risks after achieving financial freedom is overconfidence. Some homeowners begin taking excessive risks, overleveraging new investments, or ignoring basic financial discipline because they feel "safe." However, markets change, personal circumstances shift, and unexpected events still occur. Long-term wealth is preserved through discipline, not just accumulation.

It is also essential to understand that mortgage freedom does not mean you stop using debt entirely—it means you control it rather than it controlling you. Strategic debt can still be used for investments, business opportunities, or expansion, but it must always be backed by strong cash flow and conservative planning. The difference between successful and unsuccessful investors is not whether they use debt, but how responsibly they manage it.

A final mindset shift is recognizing that time becomes more valuable than money after mortgage freedom. Many people initially focus entirely on financial metrics, but the true reward is freedom of time and choice. Once housing pressure is removed, you gain the ability to decide how you spend your days. That freedom is often more powerful than the financial savings themselves. It allows you to prioritize health, relationships, purpose, and experiences in ways that were previously constrained. Ultimately, mortgage freedom is not an endpoint—it is a platform. It is the foundation that allows everything else in life to expand. The homeowners who succeed long term are those who treat it as the beginning of a new phase rather than the end of a journey. They continue building, refining, investing, and protecting what they have created.

If there is one final message from this entire series, it is this: financial freedom is not created by income alone, but by structure, discipline, and intelligent use of assets. A mortgage can either be a lifelong burden or a temporary phase in a larger wealth-building system. When used strategically through rental income, house hacking, and disciplined financial planning, it becomes something far more powerful—it becomes the first step toward true financial independence.

The Complete Mortgage Freedom Transformation

This example shows the full transformation of a homeowner using house hacking and mortgage acceleration strategies over time. The homeowner buys a $600,000 property with a 10%

down payment and a $540,000 mortgage at 6.25% interest. The total monthly cost of owning the home, including mortgage, taxes, insurance, and maintenance, is about $4,730.

To reduce their housing cost, the homeowner rents out part of the property. They earn $1,800 per month from a basement unit and $900 per month from renting a room, for a total of $2,700 in rental income. This reduces their real out-of-pocket housing cost to about $2,030 per month, making the home much more affordable to hold.

With the savings created from house hacking and income, the homeowner adds an extra $1,500 per month toward the mortgage. This increases their total payment to about $4,830 per month, which dramatically speeds up repayment. Instead of taking 30 years, the mortgage is paid off in about 14 years.

After about 7 years, rental income increases as rents rise. The basement unit increases to $2,300 and the room rental increases to $1,200, bringing total rental income to $3,500 per month. At this point, the homeowner's effective housing cost drops even further to about $1,230 per month while still building equity.

Over the long term, the property appreciates from $600,000 to about $1,050,000, and the mortgage is completely eliminated. Once the mortgage is gone, the homeowner now earns about $3,500 per month in rental income with only about $2,000 in expenses, creating a net positive cash flow of about $1,500 per month, or $18,000 per year.

The key lesson is that house hacking combined with disciplined extra payments can completely transform a financial situation. Over time, the homeowner goes from carrying a large mortgage burden to owning a valuable asset outright that produces ongoing cash flow, reduced living costs, and long-term financial freedom.

Mortgage freedom is not just about eliminating debt. It is about transforming a property into a long-term income-producing asset that continues generating wealth long after the loan is gone. The combination of house hacking, rental income, disciplined payments, and long-term planning creates *a financial system that supports freedom, stability, and generational wealth.*

www.ingramcontent.com/pod-product-compliance
Lightning Source LLC
LaVergne TN
LVHW040520210926
848480LV00007BA/1527